THE MILLENNIAL MINDSET

THE MILLENNIAL MINDSET

Unraveling Fact from Fiction

**Regina Luttrell and
Karen McGrath**

ROWMAN & LITTLEFIELD
Lanham • Boulder • New York • London

Published by Rowman & Littlefield
A wholly owned subsidiary of
The Rowman & Littlefield Publishing Group, Inc.
4501 Forbes Boulevard, Suite 200, Lanham, Maryland 20706
www.rowman.com

Unit A, Whitacre Mews, 26-34 Stannary Street, London SE11 4AB

British Library Cataloguing in Publication Information Available

Library of Congress Cataloging-in-Publication Data

The hardback edition of this book was previously cataloged by the Library of
Congress as follows:

Names: Luttrell, Regina, 1975- author.
Title: The millennial mindset : unraveling fact from fiction / Regina Luttrell
 and Karen McGrath.
Description: Lanham : Rowman & Littlefield, 2016. | Includes bibliographical
 references and index.
Identifiers: LCCN 2015039758 | ISBN 9781442245174 (cloth : alkaline
 paper) | ISBN 9781442245181 (electronic) | 9780810895898 (paper :
 alkaline paper)
Subjects: LCSH: Generation Y. | Youth—Psychology. | Intergenerational
 relations.
Classification: LCC HQ799.5 L87 2015 | DDC 305.2—dc23 LC record
 available at http://lccn.loc.gov/2015039758

∞™ The paper used in this publication meets the minimum requirements
of American National Standard for Information Sciences—Permanence of
Paper for Printed Library Materials, ANSI/NISO Z39.48-1992.

Printed in the United States of America

CONTENTS

FOREWORDS

In following the book's format, we asked a parent, an educator, and a manager of Millennials to offer their insights about one of the most significant generations of our time. We believe that you will see, while their experiences differ, there is one thing they have in common: they appreciate Millennials and their differences.

TATIANA N. COFFINGER, ESQ., AND A PARENT OF A MILLENNIAL

What is a Millennial? Am I a Millennial? Well, I had to Google the definition to confirm that I'm not a Millennial, but I am a mother of a Millennial. I now find myself surveying those around me to determine who fits in which generational category, be it the "Greatest," the "Baby Boomers," the "X" or the "Y." It is uncertain if I am able to correctly identify a Millennial at a glance, although there are certain characteristics that seem to stand out.

The irony is that a Millennial typically doesn't subscribe to categorical definitions. They shun stereotypes and are more open about engaging in philosophical discussion about the negative impacts of stereotypes. They are accepting of people on the whole despite race, sexuality, gender, and nationality. They applaud individuality and strive to differentiate themselves. Yet their collective desire to be open and free, accepting and unbiased, can still be reduced to a generalized grouping based on their age.

The world is a very different place for a Millennial to grow up in than has ever been experienced in our history. Technology rules the day. Information travels in the blink of an eye and the accuracy of the information need not be the primary concern. "Yesterday's news" is what was reported an hour ago, and what constitutes "news" in this era has probably raised the eyebrows of the "Greatest Generation" more than once.

Privacy means something different to Millennials. A relationship status is updated via electronic communication in an instant. Every movement is tracked via an app recording the speed and distance of a jog or noting which restaurant provided lunch. Pictures are posted on social media of every event—a wedding, a vacation, or Friday night barhopping—and are simultaneously broadcast to the world.

Conversations are captured in digital forms and often in 140 characters or less. It is hard to take back hurtful words when they are preserved in cyberspace forevermore. Sarcasm, humor, and true feelings are often misunderstood in type and the skin seems to be much thinner as a result. "Unfriending" someone becomes the method of addressing a deteriorating relationship.

Phone skills have largely gone the way of the eight-track player. Millennials do not know what an eight-track player is and have only a vague, yet growing, curiosity about vinyl. Interpersonal relationships exist in cyberspace even if sitting at the same table as the person with whom they are conversing. There are already findings related to the permanent degradation of posture of those who spend too much time with their heads down looking at and texting on a screen. Social graces are not necessary when the conversation includes Emoji and lacks full words or punctuation.

As a parent, I watch in horror as my children lack the social connections I remember from my youth. There were no "play dates" when I was a kid; you went outside, found some friends or, even if no one was around, you played. Forts were constructed. Spontaneous games of kickball, tag, or football just happened. I spent many summer afternoons lazing under a tree reading books or trying to perfect a whistle with my fingers (which I never did master). Millennial children met friends online as they challenged each other to video games, communicating through headsets. Millennial children also made friends through organized sports that drew similar athletes from a region, not a neighborhood. It is hard to have a pick-up game of soccer when your teammates live fifty miles away.

Millennials walk among the rest of us every day. They are not wearing any type of identification but you may recognize them when you see them. How they interact with other generations and how we accept them into our existing environments will require understanding and compromise. This generation offers refreshing thoughts, ideas, and understanding to those of us who are chronically used to resisting change. In return, those of us considered dinosaurs may offer insight into tradition, selflessness, and life at a slower pace to this younger generation.

I have had the fortunate opportunity to work with Millennials in my office as well as coaching some while they were still in high school. They have taught me many things, particularly about electronics and usually out of necessity to be able to communicate with them. I have shown them the beauty of a yellow legal pad and a pen, which does not require a plug or battery power and will never get a virus. They have shown me that the world can be pretty small as we strive to help our "neighbors" in other continents through online fundraisers. In response, I have offered them experiences that show how vast the world can be and that opportunities are limitless. Together, we have learned how to coexist while addressing the same problems with differing perspectives and solutions.

There is no blame to be afforded to this generation labeled "Millennial." Generations before them experienced the real horror of World War II or Vietnam, or even the pervasive fear associated with the Cold War. However, not since the British tried to squelch the rebellious Colonialists had an attack against Americans fallen on the continental soil until September 11, 2001. As a result, Millennials have not known the complacency earlier generations once enjoyed of traveling freely without fear. Millennials have been raised with unease and annoyance that they may fall victim to an act of terrorism, foreign or domestic, for simply going to school, shopping in a mall, or watching a movie in a cinema. Millennials live in the moment. They expect instant gratification as they are uncertain what the day may bring. We could all use a little more living instead of merely planning to live.

It seems that every generation struggles with relating to those older and younger. We all desire the basic tenants of safety, comfort, and love; the manner in which each generation provides and achieves these is what sets us apart. Learning from past experiences and having the will to explore new ideas will be the bridge between us all.

CAILIN BROWN, PHD, EDUCATOR OF MILLENNIALS

Millennials occupy a fairly high percentage of my waking hours, and some of my sleeping hours as well. By day, I share a classroom with college students, and after hours I co-parent two teenagers born during what the White House has designated as the *Millennial demographic* between 1980 and the mid-2000s. In the same way that I do not self-identify as a Baby Boomer—or as a white woman for that matter—I don't perceive of my students or my children as "Millennials."

The distinguishing characteristic of this generational group, which was born around the turn of the century at a time of extreme technological innovation, has burdened them with this unfortunate-sounding label. Aside from the term, though, this is no unfortunate group.

The diversity of this educated population, which, according to some occupies an entire third of the country's population, positions these up-and-comers to work more effectively and collaboratively as agents for change. In fact, these near digital natives embrace change, the very fabric of their environs.

Innovation is the hallmark of this generation and, while college-aged Millennials may struggle to identify a specific professional trajectory, many recognize that their career path choices are unlimited. With so many roads from which to choose, then, perhaps it is no wonder that Millennials dare to articulate what is they want in and from the workplace.

Our authors, Karen McGrath and Gina Luttrell, found that this group seeks certain freedoms and license from their employers and are not afraid to tread where this "Boomer" would not dared to have strayed in her early newspaper career. While some critics may characterize this population as entitled, perhaps the frequency with which Millennials communicate digitally plays a role in their subsequent comfort level in asking for perks in the workplace. So, although at first blush

Millennials' behaviors may seem narcissistic, as demonstrated by the preponderance of "selfies," tattoos, and piercings, these are still the same social media consumers who are savvy enough to deploy privacy settings on their social media portals. Their self-advocacy, it seems, is to be admired.

After all, Millennials often gravitate toward urban living and appear to choose between easier access to housing and transportation than they do to ownership and acquisition. Sometimes choosing to just rent or borrow a car for a day is both more efficient and economical. If more and more Millennials opt for these more practical choices, think of the potential impact on climate change.

The label *Millennial*, like all the other labels generated to tag some particular human cohort, is undignified and misleading. My experience with this generation has been marked by both instances of great satisfaction and unmitigated frustration. But I have experienced those same results since I started teaching in colleges twenty-two years ago. Eighteen to twenty-somethings and beyond arrive in our classrooms with all their individual subjectivities, their sufferings, and their joys. Performance pressures have certainly changed since the early 1990s, but essentially, college students arrive in our classrooms as freshman, mostly excited and ready to learn.

Those of us who are parents or teachers or both help our children or our students—no matter the label ascribed to them—engage with the world in which they live and with each other. While the tools to facilitate these human interactions may change, our responsibility to nurture and perhaps inspire, should not. Our homes and our classrooms may be among the last frontiers where Millennials can experiment, fail, and try again in a safe environment where risk-taking is rewarded and self-realization is central to the enterprise. Those same tenets of child-rearing and higher education have not waned with a new group of learners. Our charge is to help them navigate the changing landscape in which they are so integrally implicated and to reflect a degree of optimism they may not be afforded once they are embedded in the workforce.

RYAN SCHRAM, COO OF IZEA, MANAGER OF MILLENNIALS

It's not the plague. It's a whole new generation in the workforce.

A few weeks ago, I met with an acquaintance of mine at an industry conference. Over cocktails, she made a particularly telling confession: "Ryan, my organization has 'a case of the Millennials.'" It was as if her business had been plagued with a horrible disease. But I understood all too well what she meant.

For some businesses, this latest generation might be one of the larger managerial challenges they have faced. New factors have emerged, including the age balance of the existing workforce and expectations drawn from the type of industry the business is in. Even seemingly minor things like the design of the workplace all play a role in this time of change. Millennials' presence in the business world has been felt and it cannot be understated or ignored. This sizeable shift in the mix of our workforce is something that most organizations and leaders were simply unprepared for.

After buying her several drinks to take the edge off, I assured my friend that she was certainly not alone in navigating these generational, cultural, and organization nuances, but that I had seen both the benefits—and drawbacks—first-hand myself. In my role as Chief Operating Officer of IZEA, an online marketplace that unites content creators with brands, we chose to embrace the benefits of a Millennial-filled workplace versus "confronting" or "solving for it" as so many other companies have chosen to do. Perhaps it's because we work in the advertising technology space. Maybe it's that our CEO is only in his late thirties—a late "Gen-Xer" himself. In any event, as of the writing of this foreword, over three-quarters of my staff are categorized generationally as *Millennials*.

To my fellow executives, I provide the following observations and advice from many lessons learned in nurturing our company:

The "Mark of the Millennial": Well Educated, Energetic, Curious, Competitive

If I wrote these traits as the summary of a prospective employee, I am willing to bet that most hiring managers would leap at the chance to have that type of individual join their organization. Yet somehow the "Mark of the Millennial" has cast these otherwise positive aspects of a generation's eagerness in a negative light.

In many ways, this generation of current and future employees is no worse than their Baby Boomer parents were when they joined the workforce, having to explain to their World War II–hardened managers the desire for a new type of attire called "business casual" in the workplace and the expectation of embracing family life as part of the pace of business. Today, those asks include things ranging from creative working spaces to flex-scheduling to new types of fringe benefits aligned with the realities of being a young adult.

Looking at the day-to-day operative life of Millennials in my business, I have found several accurate and inaccurate stereotypes:

On the positive side, this is a generation that simply does not want to be a warm body punching in and punching out each business day. Instead, they want to be an active part of the workplace and company in every way they can—woven straight into the cultural fabric if possible. Companies boast proudly in fancy mission statements and mottos about diversity and inclusion, but very few know how to handle a group of new workers who not only desire to live, breathe, and bleed for a business, but who demand that their employer live up to every last word of their corporate slogans.

Yes, some Millennials were raised by "Snow-Plow Parents" to believe that they were more special than anyone else; these parents sometimes show up for their kid's first day of work or to provide moral support for an interview. (I wish I was making this up.) Others may have a distorted view of business realities and the capability—some may say "hard work"—it takes to obtain the status desired in a career.

This is a generation that hasn't always had the perfect situation; some are scarred having watched their parents get unexpectedly laid off during the recession from a company that they loved. Even in the present day, they are bombarded with Facebook and Instagram "image crafting" in which their peers post only the best parts about their lives, particularly when it comes to success.

How to Manage—Err, Lead—With Culture at the Front

For me personally, considering a Millennial's needs and desires was actually a broader exercise in evaluating what it meant to have a living, breathing corporate culture at IZEA. In other words, we try to approach every single business day with the recognition that in order to be continually competitive, reinvention will be our salvation as leaders and as team members.

Moreover, it was a learning opportunity for our senior staff to also evaluate how in-tune they were with their peers and their direct reports. We even created a senior role in the organization that served as an "ombudsman"—to borrow a term used in higher education—for our younger employees. What we discovered—sometimes painfully at first—was that in many cases, the Millennials were typecast as being "entitled" or "selfish," when in actuality, they simply needed to become more self-aware on how communication and teamwork through peer contributions in the workplace could align to individual success. Having been raised in high school and college environments where motivation was driven by one's relative performance stack-ranked against others, suddenly in the workplace, things aren't so black and white. Instead, absolute performance of a team goal became the primary mark of success. That seemingly subtle nuance required (and still requires) continuous observation and care as our company grows.

Additionally, one of the other lessons learned was providing a framework that outlined the opportunity for the diversification of career and role experiences within our company—not just rapid promotion for promotion's sake. This concept was born out of the stereotype that Millennials don't trust employers and don't have the inherit loyalty or patience required to be a good long-term employee at a business. Ultimately, our team has found that that couldn't be further from the truth. For IZEA, the monetary, cultural, and education investments we've made directly correlate to higher team member happiness, productivity, and loyalty. We knew all too well that if our organization didn't live "The IZEA Way" culture that our Millennial employees helped define and still actively govern day by day, we would be called to the carpet.

As an executive leader, I want all of my employees to stay wildly ambitious and feel fulfilled in their career, regardless of the year they were born. Boomers and Gen-Xers may soon be leaving the workplace, but the numbers don't lie: earlier this year, Millennials surpassed the outsized Baby Boomers as the United States' largest living generation.

If you haven't already, it's time to evolve your thinking, challenge your corporate ethos, and ignore the mixed messages in newspapers about managing Millennials. By quickly recognizing that this unique generation's connectivity and commitment to your business is just as strong as their desire to compete, you will unlock potential you didn't even know your organization could possess.

PREFACE

The Millennial Mindset: Unraveling Fact from Fiction aims to provide insights into the mindset of one of the most enigmatic generations in decades.

We hope what we've written is a helpful book for Millennials, their parents, educators, and future employers and co-workers. As you read the pages within, you will:

- Hear from twelve Millennials who share their views on everything from marriage and money to religion, education, and equality.
- Become familiar with the seven characteristics of Millennials. They are Confident, Connected, Committed Change Agents, Contradistinctive, Cavalier, and Collaborative.
- Decipher what's true and what's not with our fact-or-fiction approach.
- Learn ways to raise, educate, and work with this generation.

Approach this book with an open mind. Erase what you think you already know. We challenge you to consider Millennials differently. There are negative perceptions that are currently trickling through society, particularly throughout our educational system and workplace setting. We think this book is a testament to the future and the possibilities that this new generation holds.

Regina Luttrell & Karen McGrath

ACKNOWLEDGMENTS

Thank you to the following individuals, without whose contributions, this book would not have been possible: Cailin Brown, Tatiana Grant, Ryan Schram, Caitlyn Tuzzolino, Dre Brown, Kyle Derkowski, Val Granuzzo, Blake Hayes, Eddie Kadhim, Dana Lenseth, Andrea Mellendorf, Leah Rodriguez, Marissa Salzone, Ann Than, Jackson Wang, Esa Cano, and all of the survey participants who helped shape the path of this book.

REGINA LUTTRELL

To Rowman & Littlefield Publishers for once again believing in my vision and supporting this project, I am forever appreciative. My coauthor, mentor, and friend Karen, for not only jumping on this bandwagon, but for your enthusiastic support over the last thirteen years, I am eternally indebted. My Mom, Dad, family, and friends who took an interest, listened, and cheered along the way. My husband, Todd, who inspires me daily to reach for my dreams and to aim for the stars. You are such a smart, insightful first editor who always keeps me in check and never misses when to include a "that" in the right place. I would never have come so far without you by my side. To my daughters for being the shining light in my life and the inspiration for all that I do. I love you both! And of course, my furry yet fierce nine-pound watchdog and companion, Coco.

KAREN MCGRATH

I would like to thank Rowman & Littlefield Publishers for their belief in our project; the College of Saint Rose for its Professional Development Grant in support of this project; Gina Luttrell for being a great friend, colleague, motivator, believer, co-author, and co-conspirator; Todd Luttrell for his editorial eye and input; Cailin Brown for being a staunch supporter of all I do; my family for their continued support during this tenuous, yet successful, project; and our survey participants and interviewees for their insights that informed this book. I would especially like to thank my life partner and soulmate, Sean, without whose love, patience, and continued support, none of this would have been possible, and Luna who has been a calming influence during the writing process.

Part I

Millennials: Who Are They? Where Have They Been? Where Are They Going?

I

TRADITIONALISTS, BABY BOOMERS, GENERATION-X

Fact or Fiction: Generations don't understand one another; therefore, they don't get along.

CHARACTERIZING THE GENERATIONS

If we take a moment to look at some of the historical precedents and characteristics of three recent generations in the United States—Traditionalists, Baby Boomers, and Generation-X (Gen-X)—we can begin to identify and understand age-specific differences, accomplishments, and expectations of friends, family, co-workers, and educators. Historical events have shaped their beliefs, behaviors, values, and attitudes and help us to better understand how these generations will work with, struggle with, and challenge Millennials and each other.

Generations can be defined as persons who grew up in a particular era, sharing similar experiences during the first twenty to twenty-three years of their lives that ultimately shape beliefs, behaviors, values, and attitudes.[1] The length of a generation can be longer or shorter depending on general life experiences or historical events.[2] In fact, there is no scientific calculation for generational birth-year spans; they are merely approximations. Three attributes are commonly associated with the make-up of any generation: perceived membership, common beliefs and behaviors, and a common location in history.[3] These generational differences highlight an accepted set of attributes that influence how individuals falling within a certain generation make choices with regard to careers, life decisions, and consumer consumption, as well as shape laws, politics, gender, technological advances, among other factors. Clearly, not every individual will possess all of the attributes and characteristics attributed to his or her perceived generation; however, by understanding the context in which each generation was defined, we can gain insights into how best to interact with each group individually and collectively.[4] To do so, we will need to properly frame the historical events that helped shape each generation's identity and categorization.

GENERATIONAL PERSONAS

Today's global landscape is made up of an extremely diverse assortment of individuals from multiple generations, all of whom belong to distinctly different religious, ethnic, and cultural groups. Increased diversity is evident in community settings,[5] the classroom,[6] and, of course, the workforce.[7] We know that the idea that diversity within a group, including age-related diversity, can lead to effective collaboration between generations, and suggests that these groups can also learn from one another.[8]

Being able to identify with these personas can be a valuable tool toward successfully integrating the ideals and goals of various generational groups. Since historical precedents have also shaped and influenced the beliefs, behaviors, values, and attitudes of each distinct age group, it is important to acknowledge and leverage these differences in developing interpersonal relationships. Additionally, technological advances appear to be more prevalent, especially in digital advancements, and the societal and cultural shifts are more profound.

The Traditionalists' Generation

Born between the years of 1927 and 1945, Traditionalists, also known as the *Silent Generation,* are presently in their eighties and nineties. Nearly all Traditionalists are retired from the workforce, and those who remain are largely considered aging managers, often working reduced hours and involved in mentorship of younger groups of employees.[9]

Traditionalists are perceived to be thrifty, hardworking, and respectful to authority and duty—especially to their country and employer—before pleasure. Although members of this generation are steadily retiring, Traditionalists appear to remain connected, influential and, above all, affluent.[10] In other words, they are still relevant in this ever-evolving world.

To better understand how history has helped shape the Traditionalists' generational persona, it may be helpful to highlight some of the major events that occurred during their upbringing. To complete an exercise like this, we connect these world events to the following: General Observations, Economics, Gender/Race/Sexuality, Politics/Law, and Technology/Media Advances.

General Observations

Traditionalists grew up in an era bookended by two world wars, wherein radio and print periodicals were the main source of media. People were starting to concern themselves with new topics including workplace safety and Child Labor Laws, and consumer independence became an important feature of the culture, as evidenced by the birth of the Piggly Wiggly Supermarket in Memphis in 1916.[11] Additionally, the advent of cinematic films, including D. W. Griffith's *Birth of a Nation,* were influencing the norms and expectations of diverse and underrepresented groups within most societies. At the time, consumer choices were limited by the government when it came to healthcare and alcohol consumption (Prohibition), and morality was on trial as Evolution or Creationism was debated in the Scopes Trial of 1925.[12] Despite some governmental influence into the general public's behaviors (white) women were dutifully given the right to vote in 1920 under the Nineteenth Amendment.[13] Within society as a whole, the generations immediately preceding the Traditionalists had clearly defined racial and gender roles, experienced some technological advancements, and thrived economically. This was much different for the Traditionalists.

Economics

The conclusion of World War I paved the way for a strong national economy, providing many middle class Americans with an increased level of living standards. During this time, Wall Street was also thriving and the value of U.S. currency was holding strong around the world, but only until the stock market crash of 1929 and the resulting Great Depression.[14] Post–World War I economic comfort was now being replaced with bread lines, severe unemployment, and poverty for those not considered to be in the upper echelon of society. With a second World War in the not so distant future, this generation embraced the idea of *earning your place* in the world. Constant fears around the globe in the latter part of the Traditionalist era provides us with some insight into how the United States was positioning itself for the future.

Gender/Race/Sexuality

At the close of the Great Depression and into the latter part of the Traditionalist era, commonly accepted gender roles held strong. Men predominantly worked outside of the home (or were at war) while a growing number of women worked in industries that supported the war effort, including aviation and uniform manufacturing; "Rosie the Riveter" emerged as one of the iconic female images prevalent to the era.[15] However, nonwhites (e.g., Native Americans, Mexicans, Puerto Ricans, Chinese) struggled with racism despite the abolition of slavery and improved immigration and citizenship laws. Migrant workers from many Central and South American countries worked the fields but lived in deplorable conditions and were generally paid less than a livable wage. Native Americans, who still struggled for rights and citizenship, were now often used in the war effort, especially as code breakers, and their skills directly assisted the victory. Jim Crow laws were still prominent, despite the large number of African American men supporting the war effort, including the Tuskegee Airmen.[16] Sex and sexuality were still often thought about and portrayed in the language of reproduction, Christianity, and morality, while lesbians and gay men were to remain closeted during their service to the war effort. Behaviors, beliefs, values, and attitudes of acceptance of diversity were feared and condemned, and thus continued into the early Baby Boomer era.

Politics/Law

J. Edgar Hoover, in 1934, allowed FBI agents, known as *G-men,* to carry guns for the first time. Social Security was created in 1935 to assist workers in saving for retirement. Then, just before World War II, in 1937, there was a Labor Strike by the United Autoworkers, once again placing workers' rights at the forefront of a society that had just emerged from the Great Depression. Traditionalists began to look to the future and to question corporate and governmental policies imposed during this era, but also maintained a great sense of loyalty to their country as a result of multiple world wars.

Technology/Media Advances

Advances in technology and media during this era included Charles Lindbergh's 1927 trans-Atlantic flight[17] and the first motion pictures incorporating sound, known as "talkies." *The Jazz Singer* opened the door for more advancement in film and also spurred further controversy about the content and messages of film in general. Introduction of television as a viable media option at the 1939 World's Fair raised further questions about the viability of radio as a programming and news outlet; however, it was not until after World War II and into the early 1950s that TV became an affordable luxury. Not surprisingly, many older Traditionalists and pre-Traditionalists were skeptical of this new media outlet and how it might change the world.

Ultimately, experiences resulting from each of these categories aided in shaping the behaviors, attitudes, and beliefs of Traditionalists. Fears about *difference* and a lack of true understanding of economics set the tone for a continued national identity and contributed to the social identity of this generation. As witnesses to the Great Depression, Traditionalists largely consider work a privilege and firmly believe that individuals climb the corporate ladder through hard work. Leaders from this generation prefer a top-down management style and expect others to conform. They want to know that they are respected and valued for their experience and are accustomed to a work environment wherein employees are in the office, at a desk, from 8:00 a.m. to 5:00 p.m.[18] Traditionalists believe that long hours at work should be the norm, including the expectation that weekends are often considered company time and not family time.[19] They are fiercely loyal and have spent most of their careers working with only one or two employers.

Traditionalists embody the generation who oversaw the introduction of the atomic bomb, fluorescent light bulbs, FM radios, gasoline-powered lawn mowers, penicillin, bubblegum, ballpoint pens, and who survived the second World War.[20] The men of this generation worked outside the home while the wives tended to the family unit. Growing up in this era exposed this generation to a number of life-defining experiences. As a result, Traditionalists can be highly demanding, and are often the most technologically challenged of the generations that we consider. In terms of education, these individuals prefer a brick-and-mortar educational experience with a conventional professor-led lecture, rather than online or web-based educational models. Technologically speaking, Traditionalists continue to struggle to adopt new technologies and work processes, yet remain important to the more established corporations, political organizations, or industries due to their loyalty, affluence, and values. As a result, parents and guardians who grew up during this era had a profound influence on their own children during the next era that we examine: the Baby Boomers.

The Baby Boomer Generation

Baby Boomers (Boomers), born between the years 1946 and 1964, are characterized as opportunistic, possess a strong work ethic, and are open to challenging the status quo as it relates to the traditional gender roles within education and the workplace. They are responsible for both the first generation of educated women working side by side with men and the establishment of dual-career parents. In fact, work truly defines this generation, as Baby Boomers rely on the belief that their self-worth is tied directly to their work ethic. Right or wrong, they often judge others based on this principle as well. These individuals see the work–life balance as a nicety, but not truly achievable. Understandably, this can cause great tension between this and younger generations in the workforce.[21]

Boomers are remembered for their propensity to question authority; ushering in the *nuclear family* unit; and indulging in affluent lifestyle behaviors, which led to Boomers being labeled the *Me Generation*.[22] Burning flags and draft cards while fleeing to Canada to avoid the Vietnam War, bell-bottom jeans, long hippie-like hair, liberal political views, rock-n-roll, noncommittal sexual encounters, "the Pill," recreational drug experimentation, confronting authority, credit cards, television, and, yes, Tupperware are among the images that come to mind when we think about Boomers.[23] To understand how these circumstances and views came to be, we need to take a closer look at some of the major events and changes this generation experienced.

General Observations

On both a personal and professional level, this generation was particularly comfortable with bucking the common trend and walking away from longstanding relationships that no longer suited their needs. Boomers were accepting of divorce and had an increased likelihood of working for multiple companies. Making up 30 percent of the U.S. population, Boomers represent a large percentage of management positions in corporate America and may choose to work part time during their retirement years.[24] This generation embodies experimentation and an unconventional way of thinking. Soldiers returning from World War II tried to reestablish themselves within American societies, expecting that their lives would return to normal. The Cold War with the Soviet Union accelerated during this era with the threat of Communism and the United States stepping into its role as a world superpower. The United States was also facing many social changes during this time including challenges to racial, sexual, and gender barriers.

Economics

The close of World War II drove substantial economic growth in the United States as the memory of the Great Depression disappeared for this generation. Children born in 1946, the start of the Baby Boomer generation, grew up during a time when technology advanced and incomes prospered as the value of the dollar increased and they lived a better life. Companies began to take greater advantage of advertising and its role in shaping America's views on commerce. Spending increased with the introduction of the credit card and a change in perceptions of money began to grow. Financially speaking, Boomers saw an opportunity to seize each moment and delayed payment rather than delaying their gratification, as the Traditionalists had done. Although some economic recessions occurred during this period, the Boomer era was generally characterized as one of sustained economic growth.[25] Much like the emergence of the supermarket, this generation saw the emergence of the first fast food restaurants (e.g., McDonald's) and the establishment of a national highway system to keep up with the changing pace of life and recreational desires.

Gender/Race/Sexuality

As the first African American baseball player to play in Major League Baseball (MLB), Jackie Robinson, a Traditionalist, faced countless racial barriers on and off the field when he broke the baseball color line and started at first base for the Brooklyn Dodgers in 1947. This act of bravery, not only by Robinson but also the entire Dodger organization, proved successful as evidenced by the racial diversity observed in MLB today. As substantial as this step was toward establishing racial equality within sports, many other events regarding race surfaced during the Boomer era. *Brown v. The Board of Education* (1954) resulted in the Supreme Court's declaration that segregation of schools was unconstitutional, thus beginning integration. This case helped pave the way for the Court's overturning of *Plessy v. Ferguson* (1896), whereby unjust laws and racial discrimination in general became less tolerated and accepted, further stifling Jim Crow laws, especially in the South.[26] During this era, the United States experienced a number of other racial equality battles highlighted by the Montgomery Bus Boycott of 1955, the Little Rock Nine in 1957, and the emergence of nonviolent protester Martin Luther King Jr. (MLK) as an opponent to the force used by police. Support for the civil rights movement culminated with an August 1963 "March on Washington for Jobs and Freedom" with 250,000 demonstrators assembling in the National Mall, including a presidential supporter in John F. Kennedy (JFK). This generation also saw the official end to Jim Crow laws in 1964, and the continued swell of the civil rights movement throughout the Boomer era. Although discrimination toward African Americans was the main focus of demonstrations during this period, members of other races were also experiencing similar levels of discrimination. As a result, many of these discriminated groups began to advocate for the rights of all people, thus promoting the idea of a broader acceptance of gender, race, and sexual differences within society, including the rise of the lesbian, gay, bisexual, transgender (LGBT) movement of the late 1960s.

This era also brought about a shift related to gender equality—or inequality. Many Traditionalist women were not interested in returning to their prewar roles; therefore, women were also fighting for expanded rights, often paralleling the civil rights movement in many ways and becoming role models for their Boomer children. Sexual freedom was directly addressed with the controversial introduction of oral contraceptives, commonly known as "the Pill," into the pharmaceutical market in 1960, raising questions about morality and promiscuity among young women while also presenting the possibility of sex for pleasure rather than reproductive means. Premarital sex debates increased during the mid to late 1960s with the push for *free love*. Betty Friedan published *Feminine Mystique* in 1964, which led to the development of the National Organization for Women in 1966. "Second Wave" feminism challenged cultural gender assumptions. "The so-called Youth Revolution of the 1960s, for example, produced rapid changes in behavior, clothing music, entertainment, even social and sexual manner (or rather their absence)."[27] This was a time of progressive change, all under the watchful eye of a supportive president, JFK, who was integral to the expansion of the rights of so many different groups.

Politics/Law

Immediately following the close of World War II, Joseph Stalin and his Iron Curtain took hold with many countries embracing Communism, raising further fear among many Americans. In 1947, Secretary of State George Marshall called for a plan to assist in rebuilding Europe. In 1948, the Marshall Plan was implemented and provided a way for the United States to control the spread of Communism by assisting in Europe's postwar rebuilding, a humanitarian effort that led to the foreign aid policies that exist today.[28] On the homefront, Senator Joseph McCarthy, a pre-Traditionalist, drove continued fear by concerning himself with the role of Hollywood (and others) as partially responsible for the spread of Communism. McCarthy's "war on Communism" led to the unfair blacklisting of many people who ultimately lost their jobs and friends, and in some cases even took their own lives because they were identified as Communists or Communist sympathizers without much in the way of evidence. The push for patriotism and maintaining the status quo clashed with the desire for many to press for change and claim their constitutional rights.

At the executive level, four men led the nation during this era, with one being assassinated. Democrat Harry S. Truman was president for the latter part of World War II, and held this position from 1945 through 1953. Under Truman's leadership, two atomic bombs were dropped on Japan to effectively end World War II. Internationally, Truman supported the Marshall Plan. At home, he proposed the expansion of Social Security, a permanent Fair Employment Practices Act, and a public housing and slum-clearance initiative known as the *Fair Deal*. Truman was also responsible for helping negotiate the North American Treaty Organization in 1949, and sent U.S. troops to Korea in 1950.[29] Truman was a man much influenced by the spread of Communism, but was committed to rebuilding Europe and sustaining the United States as a superpower.[30] He made many difficult decisions, yet also fostered change.

Truman's presidency was followed by that of Republican and military veteran General Dwight D. Eisenhower from 1953 through 1961.[31] Eisenhower was a well-known military leader who took office using an "I Like Ike" slogan and whose military prowess enabled him to call a truce in Korea and work with the Soviet Union, and others, in unique ways. Domestically, Eisenhower assured African Americans of his desire to uphold the Supreme Court decision on desegregation and enforced this decision by sending troops to ensure its implementation. He pushed for peace and continued policies supporting both the New Deal and Fair Deal from previous administrations.[32] As a leader, Eisenhower was interested in developing peaceful solutions when possible. Individuals from the Boomer generation became accustomed to seeing leadership explore peaceful strategies as a viable alternative to war, but at the same time, were not prepared to sacrifice their feelings regarding security, change, and economic growth.

The youngest president-elect at that time, JFK took over the chief executive position from 1961 through 1963 until his assassination in Dallas, Texas, in November 1963. JFK was a military veteran and Pulitzer Prize winner (1955) who took part in the first nationally televised presidential debate with Richard Nixon and won the election to become the first Roman Catholic to take office; he championed human rights, equal rights, poverty, and peace initiatives during his presidency and supported the creation of the Peace Corps in 1961 as a way to help other countries.[33] JFK's unexpected assassination in 1963 left much of the country in tears and many Baby Boomers can still recall where they were when they first heard about his death. Even though they lost a clear champion and leader, the civil rights movement would make much progress in the years after his death.

Lyndon B. Johnson (LBJ) assumed the presidency following the assassination of JFK. Johnson survived poverty while growing up and served a short time in the Navy. This service earned him a Silver Star and he transitioned his career into politics, serving as a member of the House of Representatives, which ultimately led to his vice presidency. Johnson promoted many of Kennedy's initiatives and was reelected to a complete term in 1964 by a large margin. He supported "The Great Society" program with a focus on aid to education, attack on disease, Medicare, urban renewal, beautification, conservation, development of depressed regions, a wide-scale fight against poverty, control and prevention of crime and delinquency, and the removal of obstacles to the right to vote.[34] Leveraging experiences from his impoverished upbringing and his positions on civil rights, Johnson was another champion for change, especially for world peace. The crisis in Vietnam provided a challenging obstacle for achieving world peace, and as a result, Johnson did not run for reelection and died suddenly after leaving office.

Technology/Media Advances

With television becoming increasingly affordable, radio programming was now on the decline, with many politicians finding it troublesome to adjust to a technology that emphasized one's appearance and charisma. One can believe that Franklin D. Roosevelt might not have experienced as much political success as a leader during this era because citizens of the United States would have been able to see his weakness: his use of a wheelchair. However, we can also see how effective this medium can be for individuals who are looking to maximize their exposure. JFK was a young, handsome man, with a beautiful wife, and charisma that made for great television, especially during his televised presidential debate with Richard Nixon who struggled using this new medium. While television brought us an increase in advertising and programming sponsors, it also provided us images of Americans in space and indirectly led to the resurgence of the nuclear family after World War II. Television was prominent and influential for years to come, while radio was pressed into finding a new outlet in music, leading to the emergence of crossover legend Elvis Presley. The combination of Elvis' music, good looks, and hips brought much concern from Baby Boomers' parents, as his music was far reaching, bringing together all races and challenging Jim Crow laws and cultural assumptions about segregation.

Additionally, the environment became a topic of concern during this era, highlighted by the 1962 publication of *Silent Spring*, which "ex-

posed the hazards of the pesticide DDT, eloquently questioned humanity's faith in technological progress and helped set the stage for the
environmental movement."[35] The release of this book and a developing
parallel environmental movement in part promoted an awareness of
this important topic.

In retrospect, we can see that the Baby Boomer generation experienced the closure of the last World War, a renewal of economic growth,
a push for civil rights and equality, humanitarian efforts, the mainstreaming of new media, and the rise of environmental awareness.
Thanks to JFK, this era experienced an ideological shift from what the
country or government can do to help the people to what people can do
help their country or government. The events of this generation definitely affect the beliefs, behaviors, values, and attitudes of so many
Baby Boomers, and Gen-Xers, today.

Generation-X

Generation-X, commonly referred to as *Gen-X* is composed of individuals born between the years 1965 and the early 1980s, and is flanked by
two larger generations: the predominantly white Baby Boomers and the
highly diverse Millennials.[36] We can learn more about the beliefs, behaviors, values, and attitudes of this generation by taking a look at some
historical events that helped define the economics, diversity, politics,
and technology and media advances familiar to Gen-X.

General Observations

In a broad sense, Gen-X is the first generation we have looked at that
experienced significant corporate downsizing, enormous layoffs leading
to broad economic challenges, and widespread governmental scandals.
Gen-X children were the first to generation to grow up in double-
income, often divorced family units. Gen-Xers are often seen as a neglected generation as a result of their formative years falling within "one
of the least parented, least nurtured generations in U.S. history."[37] This
generation was the first to be raised in daycare, and nearly 40 percent
were considered "latchkey kids." As a result, it shouldn't be a surprise
that this generation is very independent, resourceful, and enterprising
by nature. Gen-Xers place family first and strive for optimum work–life
balance. They are involved in all aspects of their children's lives, and

they are ferocious advocates who demand power and decision-making rights to ensure that their children receive what they need.[38]

Those born during the earlier part of this generation grew up while the United States was involved in the Vietnam conflict and the subsequent societal protests about whether this was a war or simply a police action. Many early Baby Boomers, who were the parents of Gen-Xers, fought the draft and became activists during the 1960s. Early Gen-Xers either experienced firsthand, read about, or heard about many history-shaping events including Martin Luther King Jr.'s assassination in 1968, riots at the Democratic National Convention in Chicago, tensions between students and the National Guard at Kent State University in 1970, the Watergate hearings, an energy crisis, a presidential resignation, and homosexuality debates encompassing the entire political spectrum.

More than any previous generation, Gen-Xers are comfortable with technological advances, diversity, and have an appreciation for global issues. For example, Amazon founder Jeff Bezos, Google founders Sergey Brin and Larry Page, and the founders of YouTube are all Gen-Xers. They are members of the first generation to grow up with CDs, remote controls, cell phones, email, fax machines, computers, and the Internet. Gen-Xers contribute to the workplace as independent, resourceful, self-sufficient individuals who value both freedom and responsibility. This generation seeks out fun, yet meaningful workplaces and dislikes conformity, so much so that if they feel boxed in or pigeonholed they will not think twice about finding a new employer.[39] Gen-Xers flourish when challenged, when they are given creative freedom, and when they have autonomy.[40] This generation also values the freedom to set their own working hours and work from home when possible. Eager and ambitious to learn new skills, Gen-Xers crave training that relates to their overall careers and seek out instruction that is interactive and computer based.[41] While working in groups is accepted, individuals from this generation prefer to work using a more hands-off approach when supervising or mentoring.

Economics

As this generation was coming of age, President Nixon began to worry about the amount of gold that other countries were borrowing from the United States, leading to a policy that restricted the trade in 1971.

Additionally, the economy was starting to see signs of stress as inflation was rising and the value of the dollar was falling. Citizens began to worry about their finances and the affordability of the comforts to which they had grown accustomed. Regarding energy, specifically oil, U.S. support of Israel in 1973 led to a major crisis when the Arab members of the Organization of Petroleum Exporting Countries enforced an embargo and U.S. citizens experienced long lines at the gas pump for fear of running out of oil. The oil embargo did lead to increased attention to one of the first large-scale searches for alternative fuel sources, including solar, wind, and the Alaskan Pipeline in 1973. This push was further exacerbated by President Carter's 1977 call for conservation in his speech regarding alternative fuels and then Pennsylvania's Three-Mile Island nuclear plant troubles in 1979.[42]

Gender/Race/Sexuality

With a continued push for civil rights, the Black Panthers formed in 1966 and stood in direct contradiction to the nonviolent messages preached by MLK. Gen-Xers have witnessed great change in racial relations, highlighted by the appointment of Thurgood Marshall[43] as the first African American Supreme Court Justice in 1967. Miranda Rights[44] were established, stemming from the historical ruling involving (Ernesto) *Miranda v. Arizona* and the Fifth Amendment in 1966. During this era, immigration was prevalent, led by Mexico and Central America, wherein the United States experienced *Hispanization* introducing both cultural and political challenges. Women's rights issues were still important to this generation and included the 1973 *Roe v. Wade* ruling that secured women's rights to their own bodies, even though this topic is still debated today.[45] Women from this generation stood up to declare their rights, many of which resulted from the struggles of the Baby Boomers.

Women also fought in court and secured equality in the workplace in 1972 with the passing of the Equal Employment Opportunity Act. A few years later, in 1978, the Pregnancy Discrimination Act was passed, establishing multiple laws that contributed to increased awareness and created protections for women.[46] As the civil rights movement continued to strengthen during this era, the gay and lesbian movement was also gaining momentum and becoming more prominent. In 1969, a police raid in Greenwich Village, New York, led to riots and contributed to the formation of the LGBT rights movement, which originally included men and women; however, sexism within the movement caused women to branch out and continue to fight once again for their rights.[47] This movement took a big hit when San Francisco supervisor Harvey Milk, a vocal and openly gay politician, and Mayor George Moscone were both assassinated on November 28, 1978, by Dan White; their deaths prompted much more openness and activism, especially in the political arena.[48] Poverty was also a concern for this generation as a *war on poverty* was an important focus, especially as the unemployment rate steadily rose to 9 percent in 1975, before declining to 5.6 percent in 1979, and then rising once again.[49]

Politics/Law

The Gen-X era saw the end of the Johnson administration and the transition to the Nixon presidency, which contributed to the citizens' heightened sense of awareness regarding government corruption when Nixon resigned as president in 1974. As a result, his vice president, Gerald Ford, was sworn into office and was "confronted with almost insuperable tasks. There were the challenges of mastering inflation, reviving a depressed economy, solving chronic energy shortages, and trying to ensure world peace." President Ford pardoned Richard Nixon, and did an admirable job under less than ideal circumstances, losing his own presidential election in 1976 to Jimmy Carter.[50]

Entering the executive office as a champion of human rights and understanding the need for reform, President Carter

> dealt with the energy shortage by establishing a national energy policy and by decontrolling domestic petroleum prices to stimulate production. He prompted Government efficiency through civil service reform and proceeded with deregulation of the trucking and airline industries. He sought to improve the environment. . . . [To] increase human and social services, he created the Department of Education, bolstered the Social Security system, and appointed record numbers of women, blacks, and Hispanics to Government jobs.[51]

Carter's drive for change continued even after he left office when Ronald Reagan won the presidency in 1980. A year later, Reagan survived an attempted assassination. During Reagan's two terms as president, *Reaganomics* became a focal point. He had success in working with

Congress and "obtained legislation to stimulate economic growth, curb inflation, increase employment, and strengthen national defense. He embarked upon a course of cutting taxes and Government expenditures, refusing to deviate from it even when the strengthening of defense forces led to a large deficit," and during his second term, "obtained an overhaul of the income tax code, which eliminated many deductions and exempted millions of people with low incomes. At the end of his administration, the nation was enjoying its longest recorded period of peacetime prosperity without recession or depression."[52] In foreign affairs, despite President Reagan's labeling of the Soviet Union as the *evil empire* in the early 1980s, the Cold War with the Soviet Union ended, lessening fears that the United States had experienced for decades prior. In fact, President Reagan had a change of heart about the Soviet Union when Mikhail Gorbachev became the leader of the Soviet Union that spearheaded major reforms aimed at rebuilding a relationship with the United States.

Technology/Media Advances

As with previous generations, Gen-X experienced substantial technological advancements, many of which are directly related to the media. In 1969, NASA landed Neil Armstrong on the surface of the moon; Armstrong then uttered the famous words, "That's one small step for [a] man, one giant leap for mankind."[53] This event was miraculous for another reason as well: the role that the media, specifically television, played in broadcasting it and bringing the event into the lives of everyone with access. Television was securing its role as the primary mass medium of its time; television sets were now more affordable than ever, with expanded programming for increased entertainment. As a result, cable television became a terrific supplement to over-air broadcasting in the 1980s. Additionally, the world was introduced to the first home computers in 1977 with the introduction of the user-friendly Apple II,[54] changing the workplace and home forever. Sony introduced the Betamax videocassette recorder, followed shortly by VHS tapes from Matsushita. The technology leading to the creation of laser discs then opened the door to the possibility of the compact disk and the Walkman was introduced in 1979, allowing the possibility of portable music. Even critical foreign events such as the 1980 Iranian hostage crisis led to the creation of the news program *Nightline*.[55] This generation also saw increased health concerns from smoking, thus forcing advertisers to finally rein in their ads.

Clearly, world events, controversies, successes, and challenges all affect "generational personas" still evident today. And the speed with which change happened in the world during the Gen-Xers' childhood enables them to be the first generation to truly integrate and rely on technology and media, setting the tone for the next generation: Millennials.

2

WHO ARE MILLENNIALS?

Fact or Fiction: Millennials are a lazy, selfish, unmotivated, disrespectful, overconfident generation of individuals who not only lack any work ethic, but also can't take criticism. This generation is composed of a group of individuals that want to change everything and possess an overinflated sense of their abilities that ultimately leads to a lack of emotional intelligence.

THE MANY MONIKERS OF A MILLENNIAL

Each of us belongs to a generation that inherently shapes our beliefs, defines our experiences, and cultivates us into who we become based on experiences during our formative years. This is why the first chapter provides so much historical context. Now we provide insights into who the Millennials really are, examine some of their societal experiences, and touch on key issues, including diversity, and how each issue contributes to an evolving future. What becomes clear is that the attributed assumptions and stereotypes don't necessarily hold true in all cases, especially in those Millennials with advanced career objectives.

Some of the familiar titles associated with this generation include "GenMe," "The Entitled Generation," "Generation-Y," "NetGeneration," "GenNext," "Digital Generation," and "Echo Boom Generation." Regardless of the names bestowed on those born between approximately 1982 and 2004,[1] this group of individuals is powerful in many ways.

They are taking life by storm and changing society at an unprecedented rate, whether we like it or not. Let's take a closer look.

Many of us have encountered Millennials who are achievement-oriented and self-motivated. Although not all Millennials fit this description, many do, especially those in corporate America. They believe that they are ready to tackle any job or challenge, and do so with verve and self-esteem. These Millennials are continually seeking new challenges and tasks, sometimes requiring a change in purpose every eight to twelve months to stay focused. However, the myths that others hold about this generation do indeed stifle and challenge Millennials in different contexts, especially in the home, classroom, and workplace as they encounter individuals from other generations. Millennials are often thought of as the *entitled* group as they believe that rewards should be given to them, rather than being earned over time, simply because of who they are and what they think they add to the situation or task at hand.[2] This sense of entitlement stands in stark contrast to individuals and experiences from previous generations wherein rewards were indeed earned. Millennials are often reported to be, and report that they are, *collaborative* , yet much of this collaboration is done in the online social media worlds. They are always connected to their peers and, despite claims that they feel alone,[3] their experiences support quite the contrary. While they readily connect via social media, Millennials can, and often do, work efficiently on teams wherein they perceive themselves as equals and active team members from the outset.[4] This belief may stem from the many activities that their parents demanded they take part in after school and on weekends. By participating in various camps and sports, Millennials have typically been surrounded by their peers and are encouraged to work closely with them. As a result of this confidence in their abilities to work with others, Millennials are often perceived as brash and forthright in their desire to play such a key role so quickly; therefore, many parents, teachers, and co-workers may feel challenged or threatened by Millennials even if that is not the younger generation's intent.

A sound example of this can be found in the workplace. Co-workers from prior generations may believe that each colleague should earn a spot on the team over time. Equality in the workplace and expectations for professional development definitely differ for the Millennial generation. This means that many companies may need to address and challenge different generations of co-workers to positively work together when conflicts arise between them. Conflict management training may be needed for all involved. But this isn't just the case in the workplace as we also witness this in many classrooms. Millennials are constantly pushing teachers at all levels to rethink the ways in which they teach and connect with students. Longstanding, tenured teachers are forced to seek alternative ways to engage students with course material, including co-creating learning opportunities or using social media and computer applications in productive ways. While generational differences have always existed, for the first time in the history of our nation, we have four, and even sometimes five generations living and working together. So what can be done or how can we help? First, we need to understand and acknowledge Millennials' varied experiences.

MILLENNIAL EXPERIENCES

Millennials are nearly 80 million in number[5] and typically known to be close to their parents and teachers.[6] Even when this generation leaves home for college, they tend to stay close and connected to their parents, normally via texting or social media. No other generation in history has exhibited these traits to the degree that Millennials do. However, if we think about it, this circumstance makes some sense because many of their parents are Gen-Xers who were members of the latchkey generation and taught to be independent at an early age, so they are making up for what they may have lost. Some have expressed that members of the Millennial generation demonstrate the same ideals and principles associated with the workplace and classroom that began with Baby Boomers and even Generation-X.[7] In contrast, others believe that they most mirror the Traditionalist generation because they display a similar "I can do anything" attitude and are ready to change the world in positive ways.[8] Regardless of the comparisons with other generations, Millennials are somewhat unique and we must encourage them to meet us at least halfway in order to live, learn, and work together.

WHAT CAN PREVIOUS GENERATIONS DO?

Parents of Millennials are tuned in, available, and focused on the success of their children's lives. This is evident in the way that they shuttle
children from one activity to the next and expect to be able to contact
them any hour of the day. At times, some parents of Millennials have
been criticized for overscheduling, even to the point of being called
overbearing, and we know that there has been a 37 percent decrease in
unstructured free time among children ages three to twelve years old
within this generation.[9] Many parents have their children in early
morning classes, after-school programs, and even summer sessions.
With that being said, this parenting style has led many Millennials to
believe they will be generally successful both financially and in life.[10]
Additionally, these parents want to encourage independence, but often
fail to note how their behaviors and expectations counter that desire in
Millennials.

Many Millennials also grew up with a heightened focus on education
and recognize its value and necessity in becoming successful. They are a
generation more widely exposed to a broader degree of diversity (e.g.,
gender, race, and sexual orientation), and subsequently, many are generally more tolerant of differences within the human race. In fact, 60
percent of Millennials between the ages of eighteen and twenty-nine
have acknowledged to being in a relationship with members of a different ethnicity, religion, or race, and the same percentage have multira-
cial friends.[11] This isn't surprising when we think that, demographically,
nearly one-third of Millennials belong to a minority group.[12] This
doesn't mean that all Millennials are fully accepting of difference, but it
does imply that many have witnessed or experienced diversity in their
own lives, or in the media, and may have learned to tolerate difference
if not fully accept it.

Another key area that individuals from prior generations need to
consider is the advancements in and availability of technology available
to Millennials. Technology, it could be argued, may be the single most
influential component in the life of a Millennial as two-thirds of Millennials have used a computer before the age of five[13] and many are often
quieted at a younger age with DVDs, TVs, smartphones, tablets, or
other electronic devices by parents who need a break. Many Gen-Xers
and late Baby Boomers were raised on TV, and now there are more

devices than ever to assist parents in calming their children or providing an alternate route of entertainment. By far, the largest advances that the Millennial generation has experienced include the advent of the Internet and the resulting evolution of the digital world. Computers, laptops, and tablets have boosted technological confidence, while the Internet has broken down countless barriers in allowing Millennials to find and create their own online presence, often with their parents' blessing. However, when children are more tech-savvy than their Baby Boomer and Gen-X parents, and when they are often left to their own devices, they find themselves in harm's way; this could include something as simple as losing sleep as eight in ten Millennials revealed that they sleep with a cell phone nightly so they are able to monitor texts, phone calls, emails, and what's happening online.[14] Technology has consumed every part of their lives and contributed to the development of an innate ability to multitask—a trait many employers favor but that many parents and teachers are frustrated by. Because of their connections to the world via a multitude of digital avenues, Millennials have also had unprecedented access to world crises, pornography,[15] tragic shootings, and all flavors of other global events.

The accessibility of digital platforms via mass and social media has provided Millennials an opportunity to discover events that previous generations may have never had access to outside of the traditional media outlets of TV, radio, print media, or for early Gen-Xers, email. Millennials, not unlike prior generations, have grown up during a time when notable global events have occurred and contributed to the molding of their beliefs, attitudes, and behavior. Events like the Columbine shootings in 1999; the tragic events of September 11, 2001; the downturn of the economy in 2008; widespread globalization; and even the introduction and mainstreaming of mobile phones, video games, and cable TV all contributed in some degree toward shaping this generation. The knowledge and technological gaps between the youngest generation and us (the authors being Gen-Xers) are continually growing larger. Parents and others need to continue to evolve and become increasingly tech-savvy and media literate. Monitoring their children's technological lives is a good place to start. Parents must also learn along *with* their children by taking a more active role in their media use and incorporating technology into the home and family. We must all work harder to understand the next generations, while at the same time remaining relevant in the home, classroom, and workplace.[16] The question becomes: How can we come to understand this Millennial generation when their views on education, careers, religion, and diversity differ so much from historical and societal norms? The classroom, as unlikely as it may seem, offers some suggestions.

MY EDUCATION, MY WAY

Today's technology-savvy generation values the ability to use the Internet to create a self-paced, customized, and on-demand learning path inclusive of multiple variations of interactive, social, and self-publishing media tools.[17] This ideology is moving educators to enter a new phase in teaching with a shift toward increasingly student-centered, technologically rich, socially fertile environments that promise breakthroughs across the educational spectrum.[18] Today's learners have had unprecedented access to the media in ways the previous generations never experienced. With video gaming, instant messaging, and the pervasive influence of interactive media, nearly nine out of ten U.S. teens regularly access the Internet, and more than half go online daily.[19] With this in mind, it should not come as a surprise that instruction for this generation is becoming more dynamic. Teachers are the link between instructional procedures and students' learning. In this environment students are encouraged to be creative and critical thinkers,[20] and many have embraced this opportunity. We are not suggesting that teachers should bow to every student demand or preference. Instead, we are suggesting that there may be ways for multiple generations to work together toward a common goal: learning. Despite students' confidence and intelligence, they may not always be aware of what is best for them. They can't often distinguish between a *need* and a *want* in their education and see the goal as graduation. However, teachers often have a longer term goal in mind: preparation for life and perhaps even lifelong learning. Consequently, teachers can engage students in ways that help all parties achieve their goals, although some of these may seem uncomfortable at first. Before exploring these suggestions for classroom learning, we offer a brief discussion on *smartness* and Millennials.

There is some evidence suggesting that Millennials may be one of the smartest generations ever and, of course, some of this evidence is soundly based on fact.[21] Between 1997 and 2005, the number of students taking advanced placement exams more than doubled, and raw IQ scores have increased by three points since World War II. As a result, a larger number of students today are enrolled in undergraduate programs than ever before with more considering attending graduate programs.[22] While some of these increases have been realized because of the economic pressures prevalent today, many Millennials also have the support, financial or otherwise, to pursue their education further. An analysis of education trends by gender highlights that female Millennials surpass male Millennials in graduating from, or even attending, college.[23] This role reversal first occurred among Gen-Xers, but Millennials have far surpassed that milestone. Millennials often rationalize that being smart is a good trait to possess and these learners see themselves as part of the success of the future. Even though the increased focus for a student to be successful may have led to more students earning As, it may, in some instances, be a direct result of their parents advocating on their behalf for grade changes. It could also be attributed to the fact that grade inflation has increased over time or that opportunities for early childhood education have advanced student learning from a much younger age than ever previously experienced (e.g., daycare, preschool, pre-K). Simply take a look at all of the educational tools that are now readily available that focus on child development from birth. The goal is to raise smart children, while also taking an active role in their education, although not all parents can afford either the time or the money that it takes to raise their children with these advantages. Despite the scientific claims about overstimulation,[24] many Millennials have been raised to be the smartest—and many will let you know it.

As a result of the influences of early training and expectations for education, the burden of understanding Millennial learning styles falls to educators who have relied on traditional notions of teaching that, in many cases, have become stagnant. The twentieth-century education model is centered on conventional informative practices that emphasize the acquisition of information and knowledge, rather than building on previous principles.[25] For instance, many states now pursue a "common core" educational requirement that relies on formal assessment of student learning. Today's twenty-first century student is fluent in multimedia and simulation-based settings, community-driven and experiential learning, guided monitoring and collective reflection, and personalized learning experiences.[26] These students are also expected to engage in volunteer work centered on service learning within their communities as part of their curriculum. As a result, traditional teaching styles don't always work effectively with this type of learning.

There are approaches to teaching that educators could implement when attempting to effectively teach Millennials. Co-design, co-instruction, guided learning, and inclusion of assessment beyond tests and papers are some of the primary methods that can be used.[27] Notice the use of *co-* in the first two approaches, as well as the emphasis on assessment and outcomes. Implementing these approaches means that educators must first develop learning experiences that students can personalize and achieve. For example, blogs and other technology-based projects allow students to extend beyond the classroom and into the community while applying learning or achieving outcomes. By implementing co-design within the classroom, students are then able to share their knowledge with one another and can learn from others in the classroom, not just the teacher. By allowing students to actively participate in the acquisition of knowledge, the evaluation of their work can be realized without using traditional test methods. In fact, it may also lead to the co-development of new classroom assessment measures (e.g., rubrics). Employing any of these methods within a classroom forces educators to view knowledge as collaborative—a large shift from the teaching focus of prior generations. Some see these types of approaches as a degradation of education in the classroom and question why the teacher is no longer the preeminent authority on the subject matter.[28]

Many Millennials, however, already view their teachers as equals. In many college classrooms, and even in workplace settings, the use of the salutation "Dr. Smith," or "Mr. Jones" is a thing of the past, replaced with more personal greetings. When this happens, Millennials see themselves as knowing just as much, if not more, than their professors and bosses.[29] But to this point, has there ever been a generation of teenagers that hasn't felt smarter than their parents, teachers, or co-workers? No. We believe teachers can be facilitators of the learning process and still command the respect and authority of their students. By using a top-down, "I'm in charge" approach, teachers can often become an impediment to learning for many Millennials. While Baby Boomers questioned authority, it appears that many Millennials sometimes simply throw authority out the window. However, they can, and do, appreciate productive exchanges with parents, teachers, and co-workers. If anyone thought Gen-X was demanding on entering the classroom and workforce, then, as discussed later in this chapter, they are in for a bigger surprise. Millennials, who may be even more demanding, were raised by many early Gen-Xers—and some Millennials may even bring their parents along to school and the workplace. No kidding.

WHEN'S MY PROMOTION? WHERE'S MY RAISE? GET OFF MY BACK!

Today, there is the potential for four, sometimes five, generations to be working side by side, elbow to elbow, and project to project in many corporate settings. With varying personality traits, work ethics, aptitudes, and attitudes toward dedication to an employer, one can imagine the struggles that companies face. Millennials are blunt, techno-savvy individuals who believe that education is a key to success, technology is an engrained part of life, and diversity and social responsibility are paramount. Characterized as a generation that expects the world by twenty-seven years old, Millennials are not inclined to climb the corporate ladder, but rather create their own path to success.[30] Not surprisingly, young people in the workforce today are mostly dissatisfied with what they earn for their efforts. A mere 31 percent of Millennials believe that they earn enough money to support the lifestyle that they want, but that doesn't mean that their outlook on the future is dismal.[31] Millennials fully believe that they can increase their earning potential. One way to accomplish this is to branch out and start their own businesses, while another is to play a meaningful role in the workplace. What's more is that Millennials expect to contribute positively and take part in meaningful projects immediately. The important word here is *meaningful*. Committed to producing high-quality results, this generation expects the same from others. They want their co-workers to be just as motivated as they are regarding success. Having been set back by the recession, and because Millennials are so driven by success, many will enter the workforce with experiences gained from multiple internships under their belt. They want to prove they are the smartest, most qualified, and best applicants for the position.

Let's not forget about happiness, though. Being happy in a job is one of the most important factors for Millennials, and it seems it is embedded in their DNA. This generation of workers is far more likely than older workers to switch careers or change employers regularly.[32] Often seen as "job hoppers," approximately 61 percent of Millennials will find a new place of employment after only one year if they deem the position detrimental to their careers, futures, or desires to achieve something better.[33] Being a generation of assumed multitaskers, they are adept at juggling email, multiple assignments, and screening phone calls—all while trolling the Internet. If they feel caged, unhappy, or disinterested, Millennials will challenge the companies that they work for, and their co-workers must be prepared for this. Baby Boomers placed a high degree of priority on their careers and *lived to work* while Millennials *work to live,* with most interested in developing a work–life balance that accommodates their family and personal lifestyles first. They actively seek out jobs that promote flexibility, telecommuting options, and the ability to work part time or leave the workforce temporarily when they become parents.[34] Members of this generation want to contribute to the companies they work for, but are also self-reliant and independent. This means they are prepared to seek other options as often as necessary.

Being the children of predominantly Generation-X parents who were part of the "latchkey" era, Millennials have been taught to be self-confident. Employers and co-workers can sometimes interpret their independent nature as off-putting. Managers are often heard complaining that Millennials don't want to be told what to do, when in fact they ultimately desire constant feedback.[35] However, the feedback needs to be clear and frequent—daily at times—and managers must demonstrate their support. Millennials do not want to feel confined, demand some workplace freedom, and require flexibility to get the task done in their own way and at their own pace. They will meet imposed deadlines that are clearly defined and unambiguous. Consequently, many Baby Boomers and Traditionalists struggle with their demands and are easily frustrated, often seeking to avoid Millennials in the workplace. But as we all know, Millennials are persistent.

While they value working independently, Millennials also desire collaborative work but not in the same ways as others. They want to use the experiences of others to help them with their projects and careers, and they want to be acknowledged for their work, independent from their co-workers. This can sometimes be negatively perceived since many of their co-workers may view them as not having the ability to figure something out on their own but then claiming a "victory" of sorts through recognition of their work. But this is not the case at all, which is why managers often find overseeing Millennials wearisome and challenging. Just as educators are learning how to reach this generation in the classroom, managers must also learn how to effectively lead this generation of workers because "Generation Y is much less likely to respond to the traditional command-and-control type of management still popular in much of today's workforce."[36] When a generation of Millennials has grown up questioning parents, they will also feel comfortable questioning employers. Rather than merely assigning work, managers must be more hands-on and flexible to plan ahead for trial and error; the need for collaboration and continuous feedback is essential. Gone are the days of simply assigning an employee a task and expecting the completed project at the specified deadline. Today's managers must learn how to actively participate in the career success of their staff, which requires engagement on all levels. Millennials will be more productive, successful, and loyal to a company if they see themselves connected to the organization; have the ability to solve problems with colleagues; feel valued, respected, and rewarded; and develop social and professional relationships within the company.[37]

The reality is that Millennials were brought up receiving constant feedback and recognition from teachers, parents, and coaches.[38] If Millennials feel that they have little or no communication and feedback from their supervisor, they will feel lost and disconnected from the organization. Millennials need to understand their progression throughout the process, be rewarded for good work, and enjoy being praised publicly. The "look at me" generation likes to be noticed and acknowledged for jobs well done no matter their age, race, or gender. In fact, Millennials sometime want recognition for being unique or different from others and this desire to accept or tolerate difference appears in many forms.

MARRIED, SINGLE, GAY, STRAIGHT, REPUBLICAN, DEMOCRAT, BLACK, HISPANIC—WHO REALLY CARES?

Millennials are markedly different from previous generations, specifically with respect to living arrangements and makeup. As previously noted, this generation is more ethnically and racially diverse than previous generations. Many are also more highly educated and prone to settle down later in life. They usually don't subscribe to a single mindset with respect to gender, partisanship, race, religious association, or sexual preferences. They have been taught to "do their own thing" throughout their lives.[39] So it should come as no surprise that they don't necessarily follow in their parents' footsteps as many previous generations did. For example, in a political sense, even if a Millennials' parents considered themselves Republicans, a member of this generation isn't necessarily going to be Republican just because there is precedent. If their parents frown on interracial relationships, then they may embrace them. If they grew up Baptist, they may try Buddhism or Catholicism, or no form of organized religion at all. This is not simply an act of rebellion; Millennials are experiencing and learning about differences in their lives as more people challenge mainstream cultural norms in public arenas. The advent and adoption of the Internet has provided quite the canvas for this generation to experience these variation of opinions on a twenty-four-hour, global timescale. In the 1960s, when many Baby Boomers were fighting for women's; lesbian, gay, bisexual, transgender, transsexual, and queer (LGBTQ); and racial rights, magazines, music, and TV were the primary vehicles for expression and activism. Today, Twitter, Facebook, Snapchat, Instagram, and other social media sites allow for instantaneous access to news, while privacy is no longer guaranteed in a world that is always on, and expressions of difference are often trending!

Moreover, unlike Baby Boomers who grew up in fairly homogeneous settings, Millennials have had a much greater exposure to diversity as 37 percent of all kindergartners in 1997 were nonwhite.[40] If any of those children attended school in a major city such as New York City or Los Angeles, they could have been exposed to more than one hundred languages among their classmates. In 2014, Latinos surpassed whites as the largest racial/ethnic group in California and this trend is projected to follow nationally.[41] According to the Census Bureau, ethnic minorities will become the majority within the Millennials' lifetime, emphasizing the need for acceptance, not simply tolerance, of people from all walks of life.

From a young age, many Millennials were taught to see the world from a global perspective. Their largely Gen-X parents, teachers, and mentors drilled diversity's value and influence on society into them. With this affinity toward a globally diverse society, it would make sense that this generation is also more tolerant of the LGBTQ groups, as were some members of other generations. Gay rights only truly emerged after the Stonewall Riots in 1969 and many Gen-Xers were too young to participate in the gay movement until the late 1970s. However, many Baby Boomers led the way for equal rights until Gen-Xers came of age. Many Gen-Xers then raised their children with open minds and hearts toward various issues, LGBTQ rights included.

Although the topic of gay marriage has been debated for many years now, and was only recently (June 26, 2015) given legal credence by the Supreme Court in a close five-to-four decision, Millennials have shown the most distinctive set of views yet. When polled, nearly 50 percent of Millennials strongly favor the right for same sex couples to marry, and 54 percent report that they have a close friend or family member who is a member of the LGBTQ community.[42] This could be one reason for their strong support of same-sex marriage. Politically, this generation is present and aware of the issues directly affecting them. Being digital natives has also provided Millennials many opportunities to partake in "hashtag activism" via Twitter and to engage in politics via the Internet and social media. One clear example was the presidential race between Republican John McCain and Democrat Barack Obama in 2008.

POLITICS, SOCIAL MEDIA, AND MILLENNIALS

The 2008 election ushered in America's first African American president and, along with him, the next generation of voters. Nearly one-third of the Millennial generation entered the electorate to decisively support the election of Barack Obama; the support from the younger generation crossed all ethnic groups. Obama won the votes of a majority of African American (95 percent), Latino (76 percent), and younger whites (54 percent), and having digital natives share in his social media feeds may have made the difference.[43] John McCain, a Traditionalist born in 1936, had trouble reaching younger audiences while Barack Obama, a late Baby Boomer, early Gen-Xer (born in 1961), did not; his technological prowess may have won him the election as more late Gen-Xers and early Millennials relied on social media during the campaign.

Internationally, Millennials in Greece vehemently protested against the government after the most dramatic economic downfall the world has seen. Their message rang loud and true—they were not going to take the fall for irresponsible actions by international banks. Citizens of the Arab Spring voiced their anger over their economic situation, Egyptian uprisings led to great change that was chronicled on social networking sites like Twitter, and rallies in Chile and protests in Tel Aviv were all led by Millennials.[44] Clearly, the youngest generation of Millennials is not afraid to take on topics that have meaning or stand up to social norms for that matter.

RELIGION, MARRIAGE, AND MILLENNIALS

In addition to social media activism, Millennials were raised during a time when the Catholic Church was under direct scrutiny for sexual abuse by priests around the world, and while Islamic extremist groups led many global uprisings. However, unlike many members from prior generations, many Millennials are generally less apt to develop a traditional bond to any specific religion—they are generally much more open minded about investigating many religions. Many are apathetic toward religion and the strict rules on premarital sex and marriage. They are not anti-Christian, antireligion, or antimarriage, but they are, general speaking, not interested in religion or being married, and many are self-identified atheists. Many Millennials believe one's religion or spiritually is a personal choice. Millennials aren't typically judgmental toward others' decisions or beliefs related to their religious choices or whether their peers decide to marry. Approximately 65 percent of Millennials rarely or never attend any type of religious service, while only 26 percent of Millennials are married.[45] The grim statistics with regard to marriage have many misinterpreting the data. It isn't that Millennials never, ever want to get married; rather, they often choose to wait until they are financially ready.[46] In fact, the data actually illustrate that the aspiration to marry remains high, with 61 percent of people who have never been married reporting that they would like to do so someday; within the Millennial generation that number is even higher.[47] Millennials have a strong desire to have children and 75 percent of college freshmen in 2003 noted that raising a family was an important life goal.[48] Because this generation values stability, they will not jump into marriage without thinking critically about the ramifications. Career ambitions and being financially stable are important. Additionally, when Millennials marry they want their relationships to last. To Millennials, education and a steady income are paramount to having a healthy marriage; therefore, they often delay marriage until they feel that they can enter into the union successfully.

Because Millennials have been raised to question and challenge norms, it should not come as a surprise that they may question the validity of religion or object to marrying at a specified time in their lives. When it comes to religion, many Millennials feel that religion itself has blind followers who repeat dialogue rather than feel compassion and care about others.[49] Millennials often pride themselves on being free thinkers and open minded toward other views.[50] If diversity of thought or behavior is shunned by members of an organization, many Millennials explore other options that they view as more open and accepting of diversity.

THE FUTURE

It is difficult to predict the future and the overall influence that the Millennial generation will have on society. What is clear is that most Millennials will continue to fight for equality on all levels, including race, sexual orientation, and politics, despite the few well-known outliers (e.g., Dylann Storm Roof). They will continue to place an emphasis on education and having a positive influence in the world despite the negative perceptions that others may have of them or those who may not grasp, for a number of reasons, what it means to be a Millennial. What we must do is to help them become leaders and be respectful of what others bring to situations within the cultures and organizations that they are a part of. As parents, teachers, co-workers, and employers, we have a lot of work to do to close the gap across generations in order to lessen perceived divides. Let's start by creating strong leaders.

Part II

Millennials' Leadership and Characteristics

3

LEADERSHIP: THERE IS AN "I" IN *TEAM*

Fact or Fiction: Millennials don't want to be led. They only want to lead.

INSPIRING GREATNESS

Certain individuals are destined to be good leaders, each of whom exhibits distinct characteristics that are largely dependent on the leadership theory or model that they subscribe to. Within the ideals of leadership, these common traits often include the perception of power and a sense of responsibility and accountability. Consider how frequently players on a team turn to the captain to discuss a losing streak, or confront their coach, who coincidentally is the defined leader of the team. Within this structure, we know that the coaches are ultimately responsible for leading the team, but they also have the ability to empower players to make decisions, for better or for worse, on and off the field. By connecting a sports metaphor within the context of this chapter, we would like to introduce the idea of *coaching* as part of the overall leadership process and as a training topic for current and future leaders. We also explore various leadership approaches, and propose how the combination and adoption of multiple, integrated, leadership styles may prove to be the most effective in the development of successful Millennial leaders, allowing this generation to both *serve* the team or organization as well as effectively *coach* others using reverse mentoring.[1]

To frame this conversation appropriately, we refer you to our earlier discussion acknowledging that fundamental differences and beliefs exist between leaders from different generations. One fundamental question that we need to address from the outset is: What happens when our leaders believe that their coworkers or subordinates are being disrespectful of authority, when in fact they may only be looking for clarification or respectfully challenging the established practices? This outcome is often very common when discussing Millennials. This generation is considered proactive in challenging the status quo as they work to become leaders themselves. Achieving success using this approach generally involves risk and perseverance, and demands proficiency, knowledge, and skill for Millennials to succeed. It is true that the Millennial generation has achieved a higher overall level of education than many of their coworkers, and this contributes to a heightened sense of confidence in their abilities and worth over past generations. However, Millennials also believe in proving themselves and want to tackle the challenges that they face head-on, often tapping into their support networks of coworkers, parents, friends, and supervisors and bosses.

Before we can understand how to best lead and work with Millennials, let us first make sure that we understand what leadership is and explore some of the more prevalent leadership styles in the workplace today. This foundation is necessary so we can understand Millennials' behaviors and what they value most, and identify the skills necessary for multiple generations to work well together, whether at work, at home, or in the classroom.

LEADERSHIP—DEFINED

Responses to the question "What defines a leader?" generally contain a list of adjectives, nouns, and skills that are associated with the word. Terms used to describe a leader commonly include *knowledgeable, charismatic, dynamic, skillful, authoritative, demanding, iron fist, decision-maker, competent,* and so on. However, if you ask the same individuals who happen to be Traditionalists, Baby Boomers, or Gen-Xers to describe the attributes of *a Millennial Leader*, you will find that many of the positive descriptors are quickly replaced with terms like *overcon-fident, condescending, immature, irrational, scatter-brained,* and *unfo-cused.* The simple addition of the word "Millennial" often influences the interpretations provided by members of these previous generations. An important question to consider here may be "Why?" or "What is driving this perception?" There is an accepted belief that parents have been overinvolved in the Millennial generation's lives and have paved the way for their success by eliminating many of the obstacles that they may face. The phrase "Snow-Plow Parents" is often used to describe parents of Millennials and their desire to aid in clearing the path for success. This stands in stark contrast to a "Helicopter Parent" that might instead "hover" to caution a child and provide guidance without being directly involved in the process. As hard as it is to imagine, Snow-Plow Parents often accompany their children on job interviews, handle their grade discussions, and manage their interpersonal conflicts, among other interventions, to provide their child with a better opportu-nity for success. It is interesting to note that many of these Snow-Plow Parents are also Baby Boomers or Gen-Xers themselves and share a number of the same popular criticisms of the Millennial generation. These parents don't readily reflect on how their behaviors, beliefs, or values set the tone for what their children expect from those around them.

With this foundation in place, and a better understanding of the Millennial parents, let's return to the idea of leadership. As you can imagine, countless opinions could be considered when identifying a universal definition of leadership,[2,3] but for our purpose, it may be easier to start by looking at a number of recognized traits and qualities often exhibited by good leaders. Some common characteristics associat-ed with leadership include the influences that someone has in working, directing, and coaching others to achieve defined milestones. As a whole, we feel that the following definition of leadership captures many of the important characteristics that have been highlighted previously: "Leadership is a process whereby an individual influences a group of individuals to achieve a common goal."[4] This explanation does a good job simplifying a difficult definition, and also identifies key ideas such as *influence* and *common goal.*

Ideally, the role of a leader is to *affect* others and *effect* outcomes with the hopes of achieving common goals. While the preceding definition is quite simplified, the influence of a leader varies across situations and requires a better understanding of the underlying leadership approaches the specific leader subscribes to. This also helps us recognize many of the accepted skills, traits, processes, powers, and behaviors that leaders exhibit. For example, leadership experts may only focus on how some individuals are equipped from birth to become a successful leader, while others are not. Alternatively, others emphasize that leaders emerge as a byproduct of different experiences and interactions. While many Traditionalists, Baby Boomers, and Gen-Xers often believe that leadership stems solely from someone's specific title or role, such as *manager* or *CEO*, it is important to recognize that simply possessing a title does not always make a good leader. This is especially important to remember when applied to rapidly changing environments such as classrooms or boardrooms. It should also be noted that simply changing communication style does not always change the relationship between group members, nor does it allow for others to take the lead when the opportunity presents itself. In fact, some research suggests that leaders should develop and utilize varied communication styles with their subordinates to become effective leaders. With this in mind, and within the framework of today's evolving society, it may now be somewhat naïve to consider that only those with specific titles are properly trained to be leaders. Being able to draw on multiple leadership styles quickly has become an expectation among Millennials and speaks directly to the widespread development of two new leadership styles that are relevant in today's society: alternating leadership[5] and service leadership.[6] Both of these leadership styles consider people *team members* rather than *subordinates*.

We begin by exploring alternating leadership, with the understanding that this may raise suspicion from Traditionalists, Baby Boomers, and Gen-Xers who believe that assumed power roles and titles keep subordinates in their place and remind them of the hierarchy in the workplace, classroom, and home environments. Despite the fears of losing control of Millennials in these contexts, we want to encourage you, the reader, to acknowledge that your title, position, and communication effectiveness may not necessarily be better simply because you have achieved a particular position within your environment. As members of a different generation, it is important for you to fulfill strong leadership responsibilities, all the while interacting with Millennials with a team framework in mind. Incorporating these elements within your daily interactions will not only help establish a level of respect, but will also contribute toward becoming a more effective leader in general.

ALTERNATING LEADERSHIP

At this point, you may be wondering just what alternating leadership is about and why it is important. Is it about making everyone a leader? Is it about removing positions of power and simply treating everyone as an equal at all times? The answer to these questions is a resounding "No."

Alternating leadership is more about establishing common goals in the workplace, classroom, and even, at times, home, and recognizing that each person has particular strengths and weaknesses that can contribute to the achievement of common goals. This means that the new person in an organization, despite his or her age or tenure within the group, may actually contribute a higher level of expertise to a situation and even be the best person to lead the project at *this time*. It may also indicate that parents can also provide their children with opportunities to lead the family in some of their goals, such as recycling, planning a trip, cutting expenses, and so on, at *this time*. In an academic setting, this leadership style may provide an opportunity for teachers to acknowledge that students bring experiences and insights into the classroom and that asking them to assist in the learning process or direction of a learning module may actually increase their level of interest because their input is important *this time*. The idea here is that leaders emerge in various contexts based on knowledge and skills, behaviors and attitudes, and can result in increased motivation to take part in a group dynamic. The anticipation of being valued for what one contributes to the process can bring a group closer together, while also building a team focus for achieving goals. Ultimately, everyone can be valued for what she or he brings to the group.

SERVICE LEADERSHIP

Now that we have a better understanding regarding the practicalities of alternating leadership, let's take a quick look at the other leadership style that we are interested in: service leadership. Before diving into this discussion, it is important to distinguish that *service* leaders are not to be misinterpreted as *servant* leaders, who have often been described as placing "the good of followers over their own self-interests and emphasizing leader behaviours that focus on follower development and deemphasize glorification of the leader."[7] If a potential leader embraces the idea of providing a service to the organization, classroom, or family, a connection can be made that decisions and actions are decided on under this framework, to further oneself *and* others as part of a larger group. This is the cornerstone of service leadership. Leaders provide a service for the common good and take part in that process. They don't lose the sense of belonging to the group and can therefore still identify themselves and their strengths while also working *with* (service), not just *for* (servant), the group. This leadership style recognizes the importance of both the team, as well as its leader, in achieving common goals. Service leaders can still retain titles and authority within the organization, but they ultimately empower others in the organization to be leaders when their expertise is required. By then combining service leadership with the alternating leadership, a leader can effectively bring different people together for the good of the organization, classroom, or home environment.

INTEGRATING ALTERNATING AND SERVICE LEADERSHIP

When we look at incorporating elements from each of these leadership styles, we begin to see how we are moving toward a model that embraces the experiences of individuals from all generations, providing a platform for promoting a greater sense of value and respect no matter the composition of the team. Incorporating this approach allows for each member of the group to be a leader when the need arises, whether young, old, junior, or senior. A combination leader can recognize the importance of working toward a common goal and harnessing each individual's strengths to secure positive outcomes for the greater good of the group. Simply stated, this means that someone who is a leader for this project may not necessarily hold the appropriate experiences to lead the next project, or that a senior member of the class, family, or organization will always be the appropriate decision-maker. Each new project, challenge, and goal should include a reassessment of who may be the best fit to reach an expected outcome at *this time*. This reassessment would be led by the assumed leader given his or her title or role (e.g., CEO, Mom, Teacher). We don't currently know enough about "holocracy"[8] to embrace it here, but perhaps Zappos can set the pace on this front.[9]

In taking the time to consider how to incorporate a mixed leadership style to better relate to Millennials, how might this relate to the chapter's Fact or Fiction statement that Millennials do not want to be led? Millennials, as with most generations, want to feel valued for their contributions within the workplace, classroom, or the family unit. They want to be considered part of the group whether they lead or are being led. They want to be respected as group members and not considered *subordinates* in everything that they do. They want to be led and they want to lead, not one or the other. However, what this generation does need is guidance, mentoring, and coaching on how to become a good leader from those individuals who are most familiar with the group. With this in mind, let us take a look at the behaviors and expectations of Millennials and how they are best supported using a combination of alternating and service leadership.

BEHAVIORS AND EXPECTATIONS

While many believe that Millennials only want to communicate by texting, this generation actually craves in-person engagement and opportunities for face-time.[10] Millennials value the one-on-one time that they have with coworkers, superiors, teachers, and parents, especially when they feel valued and respected during those interactions. While they do enjoy positive feedback, they also recognize that receiving constructive feedback allows them to better their skillsets. Millennials demand feedback that is based on expected outcomes and not just chatter about the way that things should be done. In other words, Millennials are interested in *how* the outcome can be improved and seek ways to do so, but they also want to understand the process. This generation seeks to learn from others through open communication, and ultimately desires to work efficiently. Because they have been taught by their parents and teachers that they can succeed, Millennials have the same expectations whether in the classroom or the workplace. As a result, teachers often encounter students who are accustomed to challenging grades, content, and learning processes. It may not be a stretch to imagine that this type of expectation can easily place a teacher on the defensive.

If we move to the workplace, supervisors and coworkers often describe Millennials who are entering the workforce as pushy, overconfident, or brash; they do not appreciate Millennials' *know-it-all* attitude as the newbie in the organization. However, despite the fact that Millennials can't be solely held responsible for their beliefs and actions in these settings, they are still commonly referred to as the "Look at Me"[11] generation that has been raised by parents who liken them to, and treat them as, "friends." Many of us experience Millennials as only desiring to be noticed, but often forget that they are well-equipped to contribute to many situations right away.

It is often observed that Millennials actively seek, even demand, a work–life balance not previously experienced in the workplace or academic settings. This generation sets family and social needs as priorities and, in doing so, may be perceived as uncaring or uncommitted to their jobs or schools. However, Millennials are *working to live,* not *living to work,* which is what many previous generations have done. With this in mind, Millennials desire careers and educational experiences that provide opportunities for both personal and professional growth in unexpected ways. For example, Millennials are willing to be connected 24 hours a day to a smartphone or computer, but they are also interested in redefining the boundaries of a classroom or office so as to not be expected to be tied to a chair or a cubicle to be considered productive. Individuals from this generation view themselves as multitaskers and are highly committed to the work that they undertake, but also expect to be able to build and maintain relationships via social media when not in the classroom or at the office. Since they are more likely to check in with their social media communities and email at all hours of the day, perhaps teachers and coworkers need to begin to recognize that one does not have to be present, in-person, to be considered productive. We don't think that teachers and employers must bow to this generation's preferences, but we do think some compromises might be effective. The "Look at Me" Millennials expect leeway from others, whether in person or online, and maybe they are onto something.

It is also important to consider that this generation has grown up with many events specifically related to ethics and morality. We live in a world where rights to privacy can no longer be assumed or guaranteed, and where individuals may already possess digital footprints even before they have actually graced the world with their presence (when mom and dad post the ultrasound). We have witnessed the resignation of CEOs and members of Congress, and we have seen media outlets try people in the media before a case goes to court, all of which are constant reminders of the importance of ethical decision-making in a world that is *always on*. Millennials question decisions if the ethics of that decision are awry and like to hold themselves and others to high standards, especially where greed or abuse of power may run rampant. So, how can parents, teachers, and coworkers use this ethical framework to guide their interactions with members of this generation and make them better leaders?

They can begin by acknowledging the importance of ethics at all levels, including the ethics of interpersonal communication. If this ethical belief is integrated as a part of the classroom or corporate culture, then we can begin to create an atmosphere of alternating and service leadership centered on coaching that will allow for reverse mentoring;[12] here, younger or less experienced members of a group can assist a more senior member of a group in learning new things. What might this look like in the classroom? The workplace? The home? We offer some possibilities for teachers, coworkers, and parents regarding how to better embrace alternating and service leadership when working with Millennials.

WHAT CAN WE DO? GUIDING MILLENNIALS

At Home

From the outset, we want to make it clear that we don't, by any stretch of the imagination, claim to be parenting experts. However, when closely examining Millennials, what we can offer is some insight into who they are and how we can assist them in becoming successful leaders.

Parents generally shoulder the primary responsibilities of raising their children, with many grandparents also taking a more active role in their grandchildren's rearing in today's multigenerational households. Most households do not reflect the dynamics of the previous Boomer or Traditionalist (Silent Generation) generations. Instead, today, many are single-parent households or dual-career households, with parents working to maintain their lifestyles and satisfy their family goals. In some cases, those parents who feel an increased sense of pressure to provide for their family will sometimes commit themselves to resolving their children's conflicts on their behalf. Because many parents have not adequately prepared their children to be sufficient problem-solvers, many children today are often stymied by situations in which they feel cornered or unprepared when faced with a challenge. Many parents also feel an increased pressure to be successful within their career and therefore spend much of their time *living to work* in order to provide their children with the luxuries that they didn't, or couldn't, have when they were growing up. As we know, Millennials have often been called "entitled," and why wouldn't they feel this way? Many parents of Millennials may be considered guilty of clearing the way for their children to succeed on many levels, including a financial one. An example of this is not necessarily grounded in morality or ethics; rather, it is one of material possession and providing for others in order to "keep up with the Joneses." Exposure to this has guided Millennials into a false sense of fiscal responsibility by embracing debt for purchases, which often runs counter to the Traditionalists' belief in saving for purchases.

It should also be noted that simply feeling entitled doesn't end with material possessions. Because Millennials have been raised with messages encouraging self-esteem and confidence, many don't necessarily know how to handle a crisis on their own.[13] For example, one story tells of a first-year, female college student received a C– on her first assignment in her college class. As a result, this student broke down in tears and immediately texted her mother. Her mother responded by requesting to speak with the professor, who happened to be in the middle of the class period. The student interrupted the professor and handed over her phone saying her mother wanted to speak with him. In this case, whether urban legend or not, this student was clearly troubled by the grade but was unable to handle the situation on her own. If this parent had taken a moment during the situation to calm her daughter down, or not address the situation in the moment and asked her to finish the class, perhaps the student may have had an opportunity to reflect on how to handle this situation more appropriately. However, in this case, the student relied on her mother to handle the problem for her. The more that we can teach our children to handle conflict early on, the better prepared they will be when difficult situations arise, thus making them better leaders in the long run.

Often, Millennials feel overconfident and exhibit high self-esteem because they receive rewards for simply participating in a competition or event. Many Millennials have never had an opportunity to experience failure because their parents and teachers work from a policy of inclusion rather than exclusion. Ribbons and trophies are given to all participants of an event to ensure that nobody will feel left out. However, competition should be considered healthy and can teach children that they may not always succeed or be the best, but these lessons can build a foundation for the future. Many times, teachers hear students say, "I worked hard on this paper" and one implication of this statement is that working hard deserves a better grade, as though effort equals outcome and the reward for participating is a high grade. This is just one way they have often been set up for conflict in the classroom.

While these examples may not fit all children, one thing is clear. Parents can better prepare their children for future conflicts and strengthen their abilities to become good leaders by providing opportunities for them to solve problems on their own and put the "snow plow" away. We certainly aren't advocating that parents should stop supporting their children; rather, parents need to know when advocacy crosses a line toward negating problem-solving.

Let's be clear: Not all parents raise their children the same way or teach the same types of problem-solving solutions. Cultural differences, including gender differences, can affect the roles of parents in rearing children. Some parents don't have opportunities to "snow plow" for their children given relational, socioeconomic, and geographic, situations, among other factors, but this doesn't make them *bad* parents. Instead, they can still guide their children toward active problem solving and raise them to be good leaders. Some may never have to worry about entitlement perceptions because they were raised in a particular economic demographic or weren't expected to amount to much from the beginning. However, these students need to learn how to advocate for themselves; participating in an evolved educational experience may provide a good starting point.

Teachers

Whether they want to admit it or not, teachers need to acknowledge that the dynamics of the classroom have changed in the years since they personally progressed through the educational system. When individuals from the Traditionalist, Baby Boomer, and Gen-X generations look back at their paths through the U.S. educational system, the teacher was often viewed as the most valuable asset in the classroom. The teacher bestowed wisdom and knowledge onto the students and provided guidance throughout the learning process. The opinion that the teacher was the "Sage on the Stage" was often held by the parents of school children growing up during those generations. Regarding teaching styles, teachers generally imparted their knowledge onto students with little classroom interaction, exchange of ideas, or creativity, and students were provided a singular, passive path toward learning. If we now fast-forward to a modern classroom, we can see that the "Sage on the Stage" has generally taken a backseat to students commanding the classroom and guiding the learning process. In this learning environment, the teacher can now be considered a *coach* in the educational system. Many people within education highlight the fact that students can be more active in their daily learning environments rather than passively sit idle as a bank for depositing information.[14] Students today often feel unchallenged by the curriculum they are presented with and oppressed by their teachers. Resulting from what is often called "teaching to the test," many teachers are feeling let down by the educational system and fear repercussions when students don't perform well. However, they are finding new ways to teach "to the test" in K–12 while also motivating themselves and their students to engage the learning process differently. One way this can be accomplished is by using what is commonly referred to as the "flipped classroom," which challenges students to incorporate materials outside of the classroom as homework, and then foster (inter)activity for applying, assessing, and analyzing those materials during each class session. Instead of requesting that students read the materials on their own, they are asked to join online forums where they can, for example, achieve points or earn rewards for answering or engaging the material through a variety of media options. Teachers at all levels have experienced success when engaging students within their respective classrooms. Some educators are getting creative, even developing online games wherein students can earn points for answering questions.[15] By participating in these activities, students earn points for accuracy on online quizzes related to learning modules; however, students can't move forward in the quiz without providing a correct answer and showing their work along the way. Once students complete a module, they might then earn an opportunity to play a video game similar to the gaming app Angry Birds to use up their points. This exercise is supplemented with an additional in-class review of the materials, which helps identify other ways for students to work independently, in pairs, or in small groups to evaluate the students' understanding of the learning module. While many teachers may find this intimidating, there are educational resources available to pursue the flipped classroom as a viable option.[16,17] By including students as part of the learning process, teachers promote a leadership style of empowerment for the students, thus aligning with the alternating and service leadership focus of this chapter.

Teachers have also found an increased level of success in reaching Millennials by incorporating social media into their lessons. Many teachers believe that social media tools are distractions for students during the learning process. In acknowledging that students already use these tools for learning outside of the classroom, educators may be able to identify areas of instruction where these tools can be used effectively during class. This is not to say that we think social media chaos is a logical step. Rather, if teachers can provide students with opportunities to lead their own learning experiences, both parties may benefit. For example, when working with children in grades K–5, teachers may want to progress through Bloom's Taxonomy[18] regarding the learning process. Using social media, students may more easily visualize this progression and assist learning or provide a creative outlet for accomplishing just that.[19] As today's educational system continues to evolve, students need to feel empowered to seek alternate methods of instruction. Many students are not utilizing their creative potentials when being lectured by a teacher; rather, they may be much more engaged if asked to create their own stories using a number of applications designed for that purpose, including iMovie[20] or Storyboard Composer.[21] One key challenge in adopting a technologically based approach to learning is that there exists a digital divide between and within school districts, such that some children have limited or no access to these instruction tools. Schools and parents should be aware that there are grants available to make iPads available to all students within a classroom once they are intended to be part of the curriculum and this may help lessen the divide.[22]

It is also important to understand that teachers possess the ability to provide an active environment for students to take on leadership roles in order to foster development of these characteristics. Millennials are collaborative by nature and generally embrace any opportunity to work in teams or small groups, especially if it involves using social media. Each student needs to understand how to work well with others and identify and refine their strengths and weaknesses. Children should be encouraged at a young age to take on leadership roles that emphasize the value of all who contribute, despite any apparent differences. Providing opportunities to lead small tasks can help children develop a sense of empowerment and encourage them to be creative. Team-building with a teacher who allows for variation in the classroom may then set the tone for children to join the workforce in positive ways.

Workplace

One of the first steps that a coworker, supervisor, or boss can take when working with Millennials is to acknowledge that being new to an organization doesn't necessarily mean being new to the world. Many people, especially Traditionalists and Baby Boomers, believe that new employees to an organization must earn their place and respect before taking on leadership roles or working on projects. While there may be historical precedence to support this view, today's workplace is much more fluid and demands rapid, effective change on a daily basis. As digital natives, Millennials are readily equipped to bring their technological understandings into the workplace to foster positive change. However, this may create friction with other members of the organization. Rather than view Millennials as overconfident in this situation, coworkers and supervisors would do well to view their expertise as valuable and learn something from them, in a reverse mentoring type of role. Millennials would also be wise to acknowledge that their coworkers and supervisors also provide a large amount of knowledge and expertise to the organization that is perhaps different from their own. Millennials should also exhibit patience with individuals from previous generations who may not be as adept with technology. With that being said, other generations need to learn patience with Millennials as well. Ultimately, Millennials need to feel like they are being provided opportunities in order to develop strong working relationships. This way, each coworker can feel valued while sharing his or her expertise and work together toward achieving common goals.

Mentoring is also extremely valuable and important to Millennials. Organizations have started incorporating mentoring programs that follow a model of *anonymous mentoring*.[23,24] This type of mentoring matches senior members of the organization with newer, often younger, members. Each mentor–mentee pair communicates using a variety of internal electronic communication channels in an effort to effectively address issues and questions, but each mentor also provides feedback to the mentee to aid in his or her development as a valuable team member. Communications are anonymous so that individuals can be honest about any challenges that they are facing as part of their current work team. This method has proven to be a successful mentoring avenue within organizations; however, it must be noted that this program is essentially one-way in nature, as it doesn't allow for newer members to also mentor senior members. One criticism of the commonly accepted definition of *mentoring* is that it has traditionally been focused on guiding and advising younger colleagues within an organization. A redefinition of the word *mentoring* may be necessary to include training and advising for *all* colleagues, thereby removing the word *younger*.

If we take this one step further and continue to recognize the benefits of integrated leadership as a viable model, it is important to distinguish mentoring and coaching, especially within the workplace. Mentoring and coaching differ in that mentoring is about the entire development of a person with regard to a specific context. This term is traditionally associated with younger, less experienced individuals. Coaching, on the other hand, can also incorporate mentoring, but the focus is on the development of specific skills and knowledge required to meet specific goals. For example, in baseball, the third-base coach is considered a coach and not a mentor. The goal of this specific coach is to provide the runners on base with the knowledge required to achieve a goal: scoring runs. If the individual monitoring third base was instead called a *mentor*, she or he may spend more time discussing the team as a whole and assisting the runner or batter in becoming aware of who the players are and how they relate to each other within the framework of the team. While this may happen off the field, during the game third-base coaches have more specific goals: communicating effectively with the players to score runs. Perhaps embracing a redefined, blended approach to mentoring and coaching can provide Millennials with the right balance of skill development and organizational knowledge required to be considered valued as part of a team early on in their tenure or career. In a sense, we need to find the "me" in the context of team.[25] In fact, many Millennials fear that they are not being trained to fit into the team or become leaders.[26] This perspective can certainly evolve if a positive redefinition of mentoring occurs and coaching happens more readily on projects.

Millennials also crave one-on-one time and face-to-face meetings with coworkers. Despite their digital upbringing, they do enjoy and demand in-person interactions and seek feedback and guidance from their coworkers. They enjoy and embrace this quality time because it is structured and offers stability for them in their work environment. They desire close relationships and want to be in direct contact with people, and also view one-on-one meetings as a place to learn about networking opportunities. Additionally, they also appreciate when a coworker shows an interest in them because it increases their interest and loyalty to a person and an organization from what they experience as *spontaneous synergy*.[27]

Ultimately, any interaction that emphasizes teamwork, teambuilding, and inclusiveness appeals to Millennials. While members of older generations may struggle with the ideological differences between themselves and this generation, what is clear is that Millennials seek out new experiences and crave connections with others. They want to be noticed and are willing to work hard to earn the respect of their coworkers and supervisors. With that being said, Millennials also need to be challenged and seek out jobs that allow for proper work–life balance.

LEADERSHIP IS ACTION, NOT POSITION

This chapter touched on many topics, including the claim that Millennials don't like to be led; rather, they like to lead. However, it is important to understand that not all Millennials fit this mold and we aren't suggesting that all Millennials are prepared for the types of alternating and service leadership roles that we advocate in this chapter. We do recognize that when Millennials complete their educational journey, they need to be properly prepared for the challenges they will face in the workplace, but this doesn't mean that they will be prepared to conquer the world or succeed in all of the projects that they are assigned. It does, however, highlight how Millennials can benefit from mentoring, coaching, and reverse mentoring where they are acknowledged as capable and confident. They can learn from others' experiences while also providing their own teaching, mentoring, and coaching to others when the appropriate opportunities present themselves. We also need to remember that to be capable mentors and coaches, parents and teachers need to provide positive examples of leadership centered on valuing people's abilities and teach problem-solving to Millennials so they are prepared to be good leaders. There is a clear message of hope expressed here that individuals from all generations need to work together to conquer their differences and learn from one another at the same time. We know this isn't easy, especially when there are so many different facts and fictions about generations running rampant in the United States, and elsewhere.

4

CHARACTERISTICS 1 AND 2: CONFIDENT AND CAVALIER

Fact or Fiction: Condescending know-it-alls or curiously confident?

MORAL HIGHROADS ARE MISLEADING

You may have heard Millennials described as "disinterested," "self-indulgent," "living for the moment," or "immoral." However, prior generations have also been considered "lesser," even "degenerate," by each of their preceding generations as well. We can recall when Gen-Xers were told that they were culturally illiterate and too focused on pop culture, while purposely ignoring the traditional knowledge deemed important by their parents. We can also remember the numerous stories, as told by our mothers and fathers, late Traditionalists or early Baby Boomers, where Elvis's hips projected "unhealthy" influences on young teenagers in the early 1950s. Parents were certain that their children were being misguided and sent down a dark path by listening to rock music or dancing with their hips swaying. Moral highroads are often adopted by previous generations in determining the quality and contributions of current generations, while current generations usually develop their own standards to judge those that will follow. In taking a closer look at Millennials regarding this topic, we begin to see that they seek and advocate for change whenever possible in order to set their own paths in life, work, and school. Sometimes the ways in which they proceed on such paths may be perceived as less than honorable if not slightly culturally disruptive or illegal, but, as noted in previous chapters, not all Millennials fit the descriptions, especially when it comes to being called "cavalier." While it is certainly true that many Millennials do fit many of these generational perceptions, a closer examination of those who don't fit is required.

OUTLIERS

How often have we heard or spoken the words, "Kids these days" or "Old people are stuck in their ways" as though the present truly differs from other generations? As amazing as it may sound, there has never been a generation that has escaped criticism from its predecessor. We bolster our own generational values and beliefs by critiquing, usually negatively, the generations that come before and after us. However, this exercise should be seen as contributing to the ways in which each generation retrieves and receives information, allowing each individual an independent assessment of whether to support the negative assumptions or rebel against them. Millennials are certainly not exempt from this generalization as they are tired of hearing that their generation is "lazy," "unmotivated," "narcissistic," "condescending," "immoral," and so on. Many Millennials have turned these negative assumptions into fodder for marking their own existence. In other words, many times Millennials blatantly demonstrate these characteristics just to annoy others. For example, we have heard many parents lament the fact that their own children appear disinterested or unmotivated only to find out that their child is of superior intelligence or has done good deeds for others. Some parents even acknowledge that negative assumptions about the Millennial generation exist, but note that this generation is *different from,* and not *less than* those that came before. We believe that, while there is a subset of individuals that rightly fulfill these negative assumptions in every generation, others have every right to bolster their own positive image as a member of this generation. In fact, *different* may indeed more accurately describe this generation's attitudes, beliefs, and behaviors. After all, Millennials seem to be carving out space for themselves in the political arena through voting practices and activism, and also boast the most tolerance, even acceptance, of increased diversity (e.g., people of different races, sexualities, and genders) than previous generations. It has often been noted that, other than their Woodstock-age parents or older, most Millennials hold more progressive positions about sexuality and spirituality than ever before. A growing number of Millennials are even being labeled as "nones,"[1] which is loosely defined as being spiritual but not particularly loyal to any specific religion. In this chapter, we set out several ways in which Millennials actually fulfill the negative labels often bestowed upon them, as well as highlight their perseverance in the face of economic and political crises that have influenced their beliefs, values, and behaviors.

But before we start down that path, we need to have a quick discussion of the term *cavalier* to help contextualize this chapter. The term emerged during the 1580s and related to a "gentleman who escorts a lady" but also held the meanings of "swaggerer" or "disdainful."[2] When someone is "disdainful" she or he is considered to be "gruff," "all-knowing," or even "condescending." It should not be considered a coincidence that this term resurfaced during the 1650s as an adjective applied to an entire generation—the "Cavalier Generation," whose members weren't appreciated by their elders and were described as "reactive" and a "peer-group of pluck, materialism, and self-doubt . . . with little faith and crude ambition . . . discarded in a childhood without structure, shamed while coming of age, and pushed into adulthood with few hopes . . . fighting gamely according to their own rules."[3] With so many youth fending for themselves during this time, it is no wonder that this generation was perceived this way. They had to make their own marks and press for what they valued during a time when others may have been more preoccupied with other world events.

In today's society, the word *cavalier* is often associated with individuals or groups who may indeed be condescending know-it-alls, even if their actions stand in direct contrast to the label. As an adjective, it would appear that individuals from every generation can easily fit the bill of being "cavalier," *at times*. Not all Baby Boomers, Gen-Xers, or Millennials are always cavalier, nor were those prior to the Baby Boomers or those who will emerge after the Millennials. However, individuals engage this "cavalier" attitude when they believe they are correct, hold higher moral fiber, or have a position of power. At some point in our lives, most of us, if not all, believe that we are better than someone else in one or more capacities. It doesn't seem right that one generation should reserve the right to criticize other generations all of the time. Yes, some Millennials are cavalier; but, individuals of other generations could also be looked at through the same lens. Perhaps we should consider using the term *cavalier* in a more neutral, positive form. Here's one way to do so: to be cavalier is to defend thine kingdom like a "foot soldier" in the face of severe pressure from external sources. Many Millennials, as well as members from other generations, would then rightfully own this definition.

So are Millennials really the "second coming" of this cavalier generation? While we certainly believe there are some similarities, it might be a stretch to agree with such a universal assessment. Millennials are being raised under the guidance of Snow-Plow Parents, those parents who not only guide but also trudge in front of their children to assist them in setting what appears to be their own marks. Parents of Millennials often lead in this manner to compensate for the lack of guidance and supervision they themselves experienced. However, these same parents are also responsible for sending Millennials mixed messages that skew their self-perceptions and expectations. So why shouldn't Millennials be confident or even take risks? They have often been raised to believe someone will save them if they appear to fail.

This generalization of Millennials applied to the workplace is no different. Many cavalier Millennials often project this attitude as they are quickly thrown "into the trenches" of the workplace, especially with entry-level jobs. Millennials try to put forth a confident front, commit to their projects, and request feedback about their work as often as possible. They are loyal to the position they hold and will often work hard to make their mark in the organization; however, many expect to be promoted and quickly move up the corporate ladder. What could possibly go wrong with this mindset? Well, for starters, some may perceive this attitude of entitlement to success as irresponsible, especially without a history of hard work to support such rapid upward movement.

This also leads to a larger question: Can generational perceptions really be that different? Not really. Cycles have been identified relating to different generations dating back to 1584. What is interesting is that generations do change over time; however, similar generational patterns exist throughout history. In fact, there are common peer personalities by generation type, identifying Baby Boomers, Gen-Xers, and Millennials as *Idealists, Reactives,* and *Civics* respectively.[4] Baby Boomers, or Idealists, were perceived by their elders as wise and visionary, leading in a righteous, austere way, while nurturing others with a tight grip. This generation is generally principled, resolute, and creative, but can also be considered ruthless, selfish, and arrogant. Hmmm. It sounds like some of these descriptions are eerily similar to those associated with Millennials who are also described as overly confident (arrogant) or narcissistic (selfish). Reactives, those identified here as Gen-Xers, are portrayed as independent and competitive, perceived by Baby Boomers as survivors who were underprotected as kids and now perhaps are overprotective with their own children. This depiction closely parallels the Snow-Plow Parents (Baby Boomer and early Gen-Xers) and Latch Key kids (also Gen-Xers) whom we previously described. These individuals are practical, perceptive, and savvy, but can also be amoral and uncultured at times. Their upbringing influences these perceptions and they view Millennials as overbold (cocky) and insensitive to others (indifferent, even immoral). In short, throughout history, generations have thrived despite many of the negative labels assigned to them. Historical events also help shape how generations evolve throughout their lifetimes. Millennials today are no different in that sense. They are often perceived as disinterested and overconfident for their age, even amoral. It should be noted that Millennials' morality is not as much amoral as it is *differently* moral given the current society in which they reside. With this idea in mind, let's take a look at the Millennials' perspectives on finances, personal interactions, political views, workplace mentalities, tradition, and educational experiences.

FINANCES

Many Millennials are quite optimistic about their career earnings potential despite any adversities they may face. With the economy in recession beginning in 2008 (let's call it what it is and was), Millennials face an uphill battle to simply sustain themselves independently at the minimal level. To add to the challenges, the unemployment rate, as high as 8 percent in December 2012, did not fall below 6 percent until December 2014.[5] Students graduating college during these years often struggled to find jobs, with many returning home to live with their parents as they were unable to be financially independent. Those Millennials who were lucky enough to find work often commanded lower starting salaries due to the economic hardships that many companies faced. With the cost of living rising beyond anticipated wage earnings each year, many Millennials were not able to begin saving for their future (some are doing better now) unless required by their companies' retirement plans to do so. The recession forced many Millennials to consider lower paying jobs with greater benefits to ensure that they were at least partially covered in case of a health or family emergency. The spending habits of Millennials are generally considered to be more liberal in nature as they are accustomed to owing on many debts but envision a brighter, more lucrative, economic future.[6] On the contrary, late Baby Boomers and early Gen-Xers may tend to be more conservative when it comes to spending.

Additionally, the integration of online banking within society has also changed the ways in which Millennials approach their finances. Many Millennials don't know, or care to learn, how to balance a checkbook or even develop a budget. In a sense, they have grown up during a time when credit cards and bank withdrawals using ATMs were common banking models adopted by their parents. We have probably all heard a version of the story often recited by parents regarding a preteen child assuming that the ATM just gives money to you when you need it, regardless of whether money is deposited. Unlike earlier generations who often accompanied their parents to the bank, saw the check being deposited, and even began to wonder who this "FICA" person is, many Millennials grew up during a different banking time. In today's society, most people elect to have their paychecks directly deposited into their bank accounts. This is not to say that many Millennials are unaware that their parents have to deposit money or cash their checks; rather, they may simply struggle with basic personal finance concepts as they rely on their banks to do the work for them. For a generation that doesn't trust government and big business, Millennials sure do trust their personal banks.

PERSONAL INTERACTIONS

Millennials are accustomed to self-branding in ways that previous generations did not consider. Being connected 24/7 in an online world also means being the focus of external approval. Millennials are constantly branding themselves by incorporating social media platforms into their daily lives, including Instagram, Snapchat, Twitter, Facebook, and Linked In, among other social media sites. In a more personal sense, "looking good" includes frequenting the gym, owning the most popular brands, traveling, and making various other purchases that can be shared with their "friends" on social media. The pressures for being first or the best sometimes overrides Millennials' concerns about lacking funds or for being truly independent. Millennials have initiated changes in others areas as well. Despite the fact that older generations often perceive them as lazy and immoral, their elders must recognize that difference doesn't mean complete abandonment of traditions. Much like the initiation of Friendsgiving,[7] Millennials often embrace the beliefs and values embedded in traditions and then reshape them to fit their lifestyles. They spend so much time with their friends in person and on social media that they believe it is necessary to celebrate their friendships. Most Millennials are, then, by no means "cavalier" in their views regarding traditions. Instead, they seek to expand the original notions of said traditions and reshape them to fit their interests and lifestyles.

POLITICAL VIEWS

Millennials approach the topics of government and politics with a bit more caution and neutrality than previous generations.[8] While most Millennials tend to align themselves more democratically in elections, most don't commit to any one party and dislike partisan labels. They evaluate issues based on their core values and beliefs, which sometimes straddle party lines. Millennials don't, however, want to be labeled as *bipartisan* either. While *independent* may be a more accurate identifier, it doesn't quite excite them either. Millennials dislike political labels and try to understand what issues are most important to them in the present and vote along this basis, but may easily change their views in the future. What is clear is that many of their views on diversity, government, and marriage align more closely with those traditionally associated with the Democratic Party. Historically, the assumption was "once a Democrat/Republican, always a Democrat/Republican." While Millennials often embrace, and even initiate, change, they are willing to evolve their voting stance and allegiance to a particular candidate or party at any point. This supports the idea that Millennials are more accepting of difference and therefore align themselves with parties who may support specific platforms, many of which may even be quite controversial in nature. For example, Millennials are not necessarily interested in an increased level of control by the government and they embrace their right to privacy even if they don't find ways to support it. While Millennials make up roughly 26 percent of the voting population, only 42 percent of Millennials aged eighteen to twenty-four actually reported voting in the 2012 presidential election.[9] They could certainly benefit from being more politically active in the electoral process, and their voting numbers should increase as they begin to age. Millennials bring a strong voice to the political arena and should contribute prominently in shaping the future political landscape.

WORKPLACE MENTALITIES

It may be hard to believe, but Millennials are just as concerned about upholding many traditions in the workplace as they are in their personal lives. Yes, Millennials can be demanding and sometimes resist traditions in the workplace. However, if Baby Boomers and Gen-Xers take the time to build relationships with Millennials (and vice versa), then these generations may come to understand how some traditions may be seen as potentially stifling to creativity or corporate advancement. Millennials must strive to get to know their co-workers and employers to better understand how the organization has been shaped by traditions (e.g., policies and corporate norms). With intergenerational dialogue, discomfort with change can perhaps be replaced with vision, collaboration, and understanding. Just because things have always been done one way doesn't mean they have to be done that way for eternity. Instead of complaining about the amount of time that Millennials (and others) spend on social media during work hours, organizations can easily create and implement a social media policy to set guidelines for its use. Organizations can also identify ways to incorporate the use of social media into the organization's workday so that internal and external communication between stakeholders and employees integrate societal and technological ideas that Millennials may be accustomed to. Ultimately, if one generation refuses to engage other generations or display an openness to learning from them, workplaces will not thrive. Each generation's perceptions of prior generations' behaviors and attitudes can be mutually engaged and perhaps add to the current workplace environment.

THOUGHTS ON TRADITION

What is it about traditions that Millennials will be drawn to? Are Millennials morally suspect when they choose to live with their current partners, or raise children alone or in same-sex parental households? Prior to the late Baby Boomers' demand for "free love" in the 1960s, most young men and women were encouraged to marry young and start families quickly. Same-sex relationships were considered taboo and unlawful, and keeping one's same-sex preferences hidden was the norm. It is true that the Harlem Renaissance and other historical precedents allowed for some degree of interracial and sexual difference, but these differences were not typically incorporated into the mainstream without negative perceptions. Have Millennials become cavalier in a negative sense related to racial and sexuality issues? We don't believe so. Rather, we position Millennials as the "foot soldiers," often protecting the kingdom, which, in this case, promotes the humane and constitutional rights set forth during the founding of the United States. Many Millennials believe in the right to choose who you are, how you want to be defined, and who you can date and marry. Taboos once common prior to the civil rights movement are continuously challenged by this generation such that we have experienced the end of the Defense of Marriage Act. This doesn't mean that prejudice and discrimination are nonexistent, as hate crimes and intolerance are still present. Instead, it means that Millennials, much like late Gen-Xers, have grown up with and witnessed events that have made them generally more accepting of difference and not merely tolerant by law. At some core level, many Millennials believe in equality and justice for all people, regardless of race, religion, sexuality, or other factors.

Millennials also tend to promote the integration of individuals from different ethnic, racial, gender, and sexual orientation backgrounds into their immediate social spheres. A transgender teacher often receives more criticism and backlash from Baby Boomers and early Gen-Xers than they do from late Gen-Xers and early Millennials. Within this generation, more people are willing to embrace their identities than ever before, despite the risks (e.g., emotional, physical, economic), and do so publicly.

EDUCATIONAL EXPERIENCES

The Millennial generation is generally considered the most educated of all previous generations. They are earning, and expect to earn, college degrees and believe they should have a say in how they are educated. As mentioned in previous chapters, Millennials want to be part of the learning process and some teachers embrace this via flipped classrooms or innovative teaching strategies that include technology.[10] This generation is ready and able to learn new skills to advance their careers, and once they earn a college degree, many may choose to return for a master's degree, although not necessarily in the traditional sense. Instead, the Khan Academy and other massive open online institutions have taken over, for free. While many Millennials want to earn a formal certificate or diploma, many others are using these opportunities to learn that their newfound knowledge can be applied in their daily lives to open doors for career shifts or promotions. This may indeed be why Millennials and their parents are now calling for colleges to advocate for and initiate assessment strategies and tactics in college classrooms. Millennials want to know what their expected learning outcomes are prior to investing in a college education. This has turned Ivory Tower professors who expound their knowledge and to whom others are grateful for their expertise into something like a car mechanic; the mechanic has knowledge but the consumer decides whether to have the car fixed, take it in for routine maintenance, or buy no services at all. Millennials are not only consumers of knowledge, they also believe they have a right to change, ignore, or control the learning process. Simply stated, they demand involvement; a business model of education is grounded in higher education so that the "consumer is always right" mentality affects teaching and learning from very different positions than in previous years.[11]

As a quick review, let's reconsider the various definitions of *cavalier* and acknowledge how Millennials' expectations are different from previous generations. Initially, many Millennials are very optimistic regarding their earning potential despite any adversities that they may face. They are willing to take on four years of student loan debt with the hope of progressing into their desired fields, even if it entails moving back home or having roommates for years to come. Millennials are also looking for ways to advance quickly within their current jobs and seek opportunities to break out on their own. They have an entrepreneurial spirit and are willing to take the necessary risks to achieve their goals. Millennials also acknowledge that they had to weather the unemployment trends in the recent recession to find a job. This bodes well for the large number of Millennials already in and those entering the workplace. Unlike their Baby Boomer or early Gen-Xer parents, the idea of owning a home is not a paramount driver for this generation. With education being a primary focus, many graduates have student loan payments that may rival rent or mortgage payments. The NASDAQ reports that the average student loan is just over $25,000.[12] This makes it difficult to invest in a home, retirement, or liquid savings. Additionally, as we have seen, managing one's money is a challenge that many Millennials face, especially in a financial environment wherein credit and online banking are mainstream. Millennials also believe that they can immediately contribute in the workplace and expect to be treated as capable and competent. The self-perceptions of Millennials have been molded by their supportive parents who have "snow plowed" the way for workplace success. As weird as it may sound, the parents of Millennials may even attend a job interview with their child, often encouraging them to speak "from the hip" and disregard any potential consequences of their behaviors. Millennials may be perceived as cavalier in the negative sense, but the perception that they hold of themselves is entirely different. They are trying to make their mark in the world. To be viewed as *mere* "foot soldiers" is not as valuable as being "foot soldiers" with expertise and experience that can be used to benefit the organization and its employees. Everyone must start somewhere, but Millennials want to move more efficiently to protect themselves on multiple fronts, including the workplace.

So, what can members of other generations do to engage Millennials more positively? Simply put, they can engage them *differently* and recognize the wealth of knowledge that they can bring to various contexts and relationships. Slowing down our stereotyping process when it comes to Millennials (and vice versa) can make us more adept at cross-generational interactions and help us all to "just get along!"

5

CHARACTERISTIC 3: CONNECTED

Fact or Fiction: Millennials are connected 24/7, even in the bathroom!

MILLENNIALS REQUIRE CONNECTIVITY

The Millennial generation embodies everything that is technology oriented. Having grown up in the evolving presence of the World Wide Web, email, e-books, smartphones, and social media, the Millennials' existence continues to be molded by technology. They are the only generation that can be considered "digital natives," meaning that they haven't had to adapt to technology like other generations may have had to. Digital natives share a common culture that is not entirely defined by age, but by specific attributes and experiences that shaped their views as part of being immersed in digital technology.[1]

It may be easier to think of it this way: as children, Millennials learned to write book reports on computers while using the first online encyclopedia called *Encarta,* and within that book report they used clipart images to support their research.[2] Their love for online gaming and obsession with SimCity had roots in the first-ever game of this nature called *Oregon Trail.* This game taught users about the realities of nineteenth-century pioneer life, with gamers assuming the role of a wagon leader responsible for guiding a party of settlers on the Oregon Trail from Independence, Missouri, to Oregon's Willamette Valley in 1848.[3]

However, these advances pale in comparison to the digital leaps observed during Millennials' formative years. During the 1990s, it seemed that every topic imaginable was being introduced onto the technology scene, and this trend certainly continues even today. Websites became commonplace and offered instant access and a new world of information related to the topic of interest. Email opened a new avenue of communication and eliminated physical boundaries with its innate exchanging of digital messages. Mosaic, and now Google and Bing, transformed Internet research via browsers, while blogs allowed Millennials to differentiate themselves by providing commentary on their specific interests. The introduction of iPods changed music forever, as the demise of cassette tapes (or eight-tracks) and CDs accelerated with the shift toward digital. Pocket organizers like the Palm Pilot were quickly passed over for iPads, opening new worlds that allowed consumers to become part of the conversation from literally anywhere. The adoption of social media revolutionized how this generation defined *friends, community,* and *relationships.* In fact, Millennials use social media to create, maintain, sustain, and end relationships. This generation has seen the Internet move from being a resource with which one simply finds information to one where information is shared, where collaboration exists to connect people, and problem solving is innate. Often the creators of technology themselves, Millennials are also the early adopters and purveyors of anything new and useful. They are willing to foot the high cost of being "cutting edge," and they also try to foster change. Technology is clearly an extension of their beings, rather than a complement to their lives.

TV? NAH, HULU, NETFLIX, ROKU, OR AMAZON PRIME VIDEO!

Millennials are well known for maximizing the capabilities of their smartphones as these items often double for alarm clocks, GPS devices, news sources, search tools, gaming devices, social media hubs, creative outlets, and even entertainment. Yes, TV is a thing of the past. Back in the 1950s, life was shaped by this new phenomenon called the television. In fact, the best-selling periodical of that decade was *TV Guide.*[4] America was fascinated by sitcoms like *I Love Lucy, Father Knows*

Best, and *Leave It to Beaver* and Westerns such as *The Lone Ranger, Gunsmoke, Rawhide,* and the short-lived *Hopalong Cassidy.* The modern news broadcast was established with Edward R. Murrow's *See It Now* wherein popular headlines from the radio were transformed into TV news. Children were also introduced to Saturday morning cartoons and entertainment programming, including *The Mickey Mouse Club* and *Howdy Doody.* Today, media habits have morphed into a multitasking endeavor where one medium alone does not necessarily fulfill the experience.

When Millennials are online and connected, 53 percent are listening to music, 40 percent are talking on the phone, 24 percent are doing their homework, and 39 percent are watching television,[5] although not necessarily in the traditional sense. In fact, if you're calling it "watching TV" you're probably dating yourself, as today's Millennials generally break down the term into its specific genre: a sitcom, drama, series, or streaming movies. Over 67 percent of Millennials only watch "television" via streaming media.[6] Seventy-four percent use their computers to stream video content while 55 percent use a television or gaming system with integrated online capabilities. Additionally, 37 percent of Millennials watch "television" on tablets while 30 percent watch on smartphones.[7] Streaming has become mainstream and "distracted viewing" has also entered the conversation with 78 percent of U.S. adults reporting that they do other things while watching TV, including various online activities like reading and texting.[8]

The term *binge watching,* the act of watching multiple episodes or even a complete television series in its entirety with little interruption, is becoming a phenomenon and accepted practice. Millennials often watch between two and six episodes of the same television show in a single sitting.[9] Online media services like Hulu, Amazon Prime, and Netflix are catering to the wants of this generation. Netflix, for example, creates exclusive content for viewers.[10] If you would like to see the latest season of *Orange Is the New Black, House of Cards,* or the Academy Award–nominated movie *The Square,* then you will have to subscribe to Netflix because you won't be able to find these programs on cable (and you never will). Netflix has even joined forces with Hollywood celebrities and IMAX theaters to make available certain titles while they are simultaneously released in the theaters. The first actor to sign on with Netflix was Adam Sandler,[11] with many more following close behind. Clearly, streaming is an important part of Millennials' lives as media businesses continue to adapt to meet *their* demands, not vice versa. In fact, not only do Millennials love streaming, they also enjoy being content providers and creators.

CONTENT = CONTRIBUTION

It's not enough to read an article online, watch the nightly news, or listen to the latest release from a favorite artist on the radio anymore. Millennials have an innate need to be part of the conversation and feel entitled to do so. They like to share and communicate what they know—NOW! ShareThis, a social networking tool that allows users to interface in multiple social media outlets with a single click, recently observed the online browsing and social patterns of over fifty-eight million American Millennials over the course of a four-month period and collected "approximately 2.4 billion social signals linked to content across over 2 million websites and mobile apps."[12] Their research found that as sharers, Millennials were highly active, influential, channel agnostic, and cross-device users. They were three times more likely to share content using social networks and two times more likely to click on content shared by their peers.[13] However, different media channels hold different meanings to users from this generation. Interactions that Millennials have on Twitter differ from their interactions on Facebook, Pinterest, Instagram, and so on. More than any other age group, Millennials actively lend their voices on topics and passions that are relevant to them,[14] but their need to be part of the conversation is not entirely novel.

Millennials have been contributing to blogs for years—either maintaining their own blogs or commenting on others' blogs: They embrace the desire to create content. In fact, 58 percent of Millennials create content on a weekly basis in some form or another, while 71 percent engage with peer-created content regularly.[15] Millennials want to be part of the conversation and they want to be active contributors rather than passive bystanders. Anyone, anywhere, can write, publish, share, and promote content. Even the consumption of news has evolved into what we have come to recognize as familiar. Millennials typically access news using their smart devices, allowing them to consume desired information on their own time. For example, journalists are not the only ones who now report or record the news. While they are still part of the news reporting cycle, many headlines and new stories are derived from Internet sites, blogs, tweets, Instagram photos, and personal videos shot from a smart device. While not traditionally trained to be journalists, many of these "on the street reporters" or "recorders of events" are having their content used as part of many news stories. In 2006, CNN realized the importance of these contributions to their news and created an iReport area within their website. Anyone can submit photos, audio, and videos that are then verified by CNN staffers (although sometimes they do get it wrong, including when the news initially reported that Steve Jobs had died when he had not). Once verified, the story is published or contributes to a larger story. Since reporters can't be everywhere, and social media and smartphones can, CNN created a new version of citizen journalism that has assisted them in reporting and covering many events, including the 2007 Virginia Tech massacre, and more recently the shooting in Ferguson, Missouri, in 2014. However, keep in mind that CNN is not the only media outlet engaging readers at deeper levels.

What do the *Wall Street Journal*, CNN, the *New York Times*, Buzz-Feed, and Mashable have in common? They all give readers the ability to take part in the conversation either by providing comments or creating original content. This contribution is not limited to their main websites because information is also used on their Twitter feeds, Facebook pages, Pinterest boards, and even Instagram accounts. Users can share their reaction to the stories being reported by commenting using various social media outlets and responding with original Tweets, retweeting, or posting a photo or video of what's happening during an event.

One clear example of citizen journalism was evident in the immediate aftermath of the Boston Marathon bombing in 2013. As the news unfolded, social media users played a key role in identifying, tracking, and apprehending the Boston Marathon bombers. Social media were responsible for continuous dissemination of new information as this story developed. Smartphone photos and videos were invaluable to solving the crime.[16] *Boston Globe* staff members who were covering the event immediately began live-tweeting as events started to unravel. The *Globe* newsroom used TweetDeck, a social media management tool that aggregates messages, to manage its list of reporters who were feeding into the newspaper's live blog.[17] When an image of one of the suspects was first tweeted, it garnered more than 3,000 retweets in minutes. As the search for the bombers came to a close, citizens around Boston were tweeting what was happening outside their windows and reporters were incorporating that information into their articles.[18]

Another example of citizen contributions relates to prominent Millennial celebrity and publicity maven Taylor Swift. Swift has a great understanding of her fan base, as they are extremely eager to help her promote her latest initiatives and albums. Unlike some contemporary artists who "sneak" their new albums onto people's iTunes libraries, Taylor Swift knows what her audience wants and involves them in the excitement of the album release as appropriate. Where Swift differs from other pop stars is in the way that she empowered her fans directly. Diehard fans were invited to exclusive preview listening parties across the country, called the #1989SecretSessions, where they could hear the music and talk about it on their social networks. When the album was finally released, the Internet saw a flurry of photos, comments, and conversations centered on the events leading up to the release.[19] What is important here is that Swift understands her fan base and personalizes her message specific to them. Fans, in turn, take part in the promotion of the album and create content that fuels the rise in sales. Taylor Swift is a tech-savvy Millennial who knows how to garner publicity and increase sales.

As you can see, Millennials' need to be connected is far more integrated into their social fabric than any other preceding generation. With their cell phones and smart devices active 24/7, so as not to miss important status updates or viewing the latest Tweet, Snapchat, or Instagram photos, Millennials have an uncontrollable, even insatiable, urge to catch up on what's happening at all times. They constantly live with one foot in the real world and one foot in their online worlds.

LIVING A DOUBLE LIFE

Smart devices are an indispensable part of Millennials' lives. Recent reports indicate that smartphone adoption among American teens has substantially increased and mobile access to the Internet is pervasive.[20] Teens today are "cell-mostly" Internet users, and report that they access online applications predominantly using their smartphones and not necessarily other devices like desktop computers or laptops.[21] Thirty-seven percent of American youth ages twelve through seventeen now have a smartphone, and one in four teens uses a tablet consistently.[22] Mobile platforms allow Millennials to stay connected throughout the day, the night, and even while in the bathroom. Yes, the bathroom! A whopping 32 percent bring their phones with them into one of the most private of places.[23] Millennials tend to use their mobile devices differently from how their parents use them. Many Baby Boomers and Gen-Xers use their phones to actually *call* family and friends while Millennials often text. Previous generations also use GPS devices such as a TomTom or Garmin for directions, whereas Millennials often sync their phone's location service or use a GPS application for the same result. Many new vehicles now offer Wi-Fi, while most have USB outlets to connect different devices. So using a smartphone or tablet is not as far-reaching as it may seem. After all, many of us can remember the Shower Radio or taking our Walkman (portable cassette and CD players) into the bathroom. What this suggests is that Millennials are not the first generation to use technology in ways that seem odd to previous generations. The difference may indeed lie in the fact that the expectations for continued connectivity are much higher than before. If we consider that teens today are a barometer of the cutting-edge of mobile connectivity, we can only imagine how Neo-Millennials, or Generation-Z, will be connected.

Using a slightly different lens to further investigate technology and Millennials, a recent report examined the relationship between Millennial moms and their mobile device tendencies.[24] As a group, Millennial moms spend 76 percent of their digital time on mobile devices.[25] Millennial parents can pretty much run an entire household from a smartphone or tablet, and have in general taken the lead in new platform adoption within the digital era by utilizing the Internet, mobile technology, and social media to construct personalized networks of friends, colleagues, and affinity groups.

Another difference attributed to connectivity is how the Millennial generation is redefining friendships and relationships.[26] Within this context, friends are not necessarily limited to your neighbors, classmates, or the people that you may work with, but may include someone who retweeted something that you said, someone you met at a club or on a blog community, or even via Facebook through another friend. On average, Millennials have approximately 250 "friends" on Facebook, with Gen-Xers typically having around 200 friends. In contrast, younger Baby Boomers (forty-nine to fifty-seven years old) reported having an average of ninety-eight friends, while older Baby Boomers (fifty-eight to sixty-seven years old) and Traditionalists reported approximately fifty friends.[27] Because Millennials are constantly living in two worlds, some media pundits worry that depression and anxiety may be on the rise, while the desire to interact with people directly and develop human relationships in person is on the decline, and they aren't alone in their assertions.

According to a recent survey, Millennials are more stressed than any other current living generation.[28] Overall, Millennials, anyone between the ages of eighteen and thirty-three, reported that they had a stress level of 5.4 out of 10; a healthy stress level is 3.6. Nineteen percent of Millennials reported that they had depression compared with 14 percent of Gen-Xers, 12 percent Baby Boomers, and 11 percent of those older than sixty-seven.[29] A similar study revealed that the more people used Facebook, the worse they felt. This ultimately resulted in the rating of their overall satisfaction in life declining over time. On the other hand, direct interactions with people didn't lead to the same negative conclusions.[30] This seems to indicate that in-person human contact is still a necessity.

Highlighting the opposite view, author David Burstein, who is also a Millennial, looks at these online relationships a bit differently. In fact, he asserts that Millennials understand that having hundreds of friends on Facebook doesn't mean that they truly believe they have hundreds of friends.[31] He even cites the advertisement for the iPad 2, stating the company got it right with their promotion of the new product. The ad reads, "We'll never stop sharing our memories, or getting lost in a good book. We'll always cook dinner and cheer for our favorite team. We'll still go to meetings, make home movies, and learn new things. But how we do all this will never be the same."[32]

One implication of his observation is that perhaps social networking sites aren't *displacing* human interactions between family and friends, but rather *forging* new ways to express intimacy, friendship, and sense of community. Some might make a case that the use of social media has broadened our reach and helped families keep in touch despite the distance between them. Historically, technological advances from the printing press to the telephone were met with scrutiny and not readily embraced. However, we have seen how these technologies both contribute to and enhance our lives. The double life that Millennials live has only reinforced their stronghold in our global community. Technology has become an extension of who Millennials are as their curation of knowledge, business acumen, political information, commerce, creative activities, and human communication takes place through technology that emulates today's social sphere in an online environment. Millennials have become agile in switching their focus between their online lives and actual lives. So we must ask ourselves, "What, if anything, is this generation giving up in order to be so connected?" And, while we answer this question, we must also consider its reverse as well: "What, if anything, is this generation gaining or providing in being so connected?" We need only to look at how privacy has changed with 24/7 connectivity to assess one important characteristic that most of us have given up in our online world.

WHO NEEDS PRIVACY?

Millennials have made it a habit of personally "opening up" online more than any previous generation. They will post everything from their morning coffee to intimate photos with their significant others. When questioned about their privacy, it seems that many Millennials are utterly confused when it comes to protecting or even maintaining it, as 70 percent of Millennials agree that no one should have access to their data or online behavior, yet 25 percent are willing to give it away for more relevant advertising or better coupons.[33] When asked pointedly, Millennials do in fact say they are concerned about online privacy issues, but on the whole, very few have taken action to safeguard their privacy.[34] They just aren't ready to give up their social media or technological devices. Interestingly enough, members of this generation would rather give up their data and privacy than their Facebook pages and Twitter accounts. The authors of *Who's Spying on You?* provide an insightful, painstaking view of how privacy has changed with the adoption of technological advancements.[35] While they acknowledge just how convenient and easy these advancements make our lives, the authors also take time to highlight the areas where we are made more vulnerable on a daily basis, including computer cookies, smart refrigerators, lighting, gaming systems, and even a car's EZ-pass system used to travel major highways. Even after reading the book, many college students still report that while they are aware of the dangers and are a bit afraid, they haven't made many changes to their connected lives. One reason is that they will be missing out on something social with their peers or have to make extra efforts rather than simply load apps that help with electronics, news, trends, and location services that simplify their lives.

Shockingly, 81 percent of Millennials are eager to upload and share photos and videos of themselves in almost every situation without receiving anything in return.[36] When today's couples become engaged to be married, they often share every moment, from the ring to the "I do," with photos, videos, updates, and comments. But dangers abound, from identity theft to computer viruses, and Millennials need to wake up and smell the proverbial coffee. Lives are often shattered because of how much information is being shared. Just ask Olympic swimmer and Gold Medalist Michael Phelps or U.S. Representative of New York's Ninth District Anthony Weiner, who have both shared compromising photos and situations resulting in substantial personal scrutiny. Today, social media platforms have become platforms for sharing deeply personal (e.g., ultrasounds), sometimes painful events (e.g., car crash photos or emergency room visits) in our lives, and many Millennials find it cathartic to share everything online. Yet we are just now beginning to understand the potential ramifications of so much information being shared as evidenced by an increase in cyberbullying and cyberharassment. What is clear is that Millennials are not thinking about the future or the consequences of such sharing; they are living in the now when it comes to social media and connectivity. With that being said, awareness is growing among Millennials that posting "on the fly" may cause irreparable damage to a person's life, career, or future; however, the propensity to stop is going to take some time to develop.

This poses a number of larger questions that need to be addressed. With so much personal data being mined daily by corporations, hackers, and governments alike, it is not unrealistic to think that Millennials will be the generation responsible for shaping policies attributed to this issue; one such example is Eric Snowden. While many deplore Snowden's leaking of classified secrets about his government's national and international surveillance programs, many others applaud him for raising awareness and even protecting U.S. citizens from having their civil liberties violated. It's a conundrum for most of us to balance how governments operate, the types of information that they collect, and how they collect it, while contemplating our overall national security. While Snowden's principles guided his decision to share the information with the British newspaper *The Guardian,* we pose the question: Has the nation been put at risk? Debate on these surveillance issues and the consequences of the leaks is ongoing and continues to raise issues about government oversight. This Millennial, Snowden, certainly had an impact related to data mining in the United States.

BRAIN GAMES

We claim that media have become an extension of ourselves, and while we have come to understand that the human brain does not physically change based on outside stimulation after the age of three,[37] some suggest that what we've come to know is wrong. They believe that Millennials' brains are hard-wired differently because technology has been such an integral part of their upbringing.[38] The way in which children socialize with one another and play is immensely different from previous generations. Rather than playing outside, turning the backyard into a pirate ship, riding bikes to friends' houses, or lounging with a good book, Millennials have often been plugged in and continue to consume technology in every form. In their lifetime they have played over 10,000 hours of videogames, read and sent over 200,000 emails and instant messages, talked on mobile phones for more than 10,000 hours, watched 20,000 hours of television, and took in over 500,000 commercials.[39] With the consumption of so much technology, Millennials' brains are likely physically different as a result of the digital input they received during their formative years, and this difference leads to changes in the brain structures and affects the way people think. Furthermore, these transformations to the brain happen throughout a person's lifetime. This means that our brains are continually reorganizing throughout our childhood and adult lives, and we should challenge the brain as often as possible.

With this information, we assert that children raised on computers do in fact think differently from the rest of us, as Millennial children develop "hypertext minds" that leap around as though their cognitive structures were parallel, not sequential.[40] Even Millennial teenagers use different areas of their brain and think in different ways than adults.[41] At home, in the classroom, and at work, this has implications for anyone interacting with them. Too often, we hear that Millennials have short attention spans, but that isn't necessarily justified. Many Millennials crave interactivity and immediate responses. With the traditional forms of education or workplace settings providing a smaller degree of this type of stimulation, Millennials often carry the stigma of not paying attention.[42] We can continue to play the blame game when it comes to the reasons why Millennials are perceived as lazy or inattentive, but if we as parents, teachers, and co-workers can simply embrace that Millennials are indeed different in nature, we too may be able to adapt to them and help them adapt to us when generational differences emerge at home, in the classroom, or in the workplace.

DIGITAL NATIVES: CONCLUSION

We have seen in this chapter that Millennials embrace and treat technology like no other generation to date. As Millennials, they study, work, write, and interact with each other differently. Many will choose an e-book over a paperback, read the *New York Times* blog instead of the *New York Times* newspaper, meet a person online before they meet in person, and text before they make a phone call. All areas of their lives are governed by digital technology, from relationships to philanthropy. The digital era has forever transformed how Millennials live and relate to the world, and parents, teachers, co-workers, and employers must recognize that and work with it where they can. Millennials are a committed and connected generation that has proven to be advantageous in all areas of life and with those who live and work with this generation. We need to acknowledge this need for connectivity and learn ways to manage this need at work, in the classroom, and at home.

6

CHARACTERISTIC 4: COLLABORATIVE

Fact or Fiction: Millennials put the "I" in *team* and redefine *collaboration.*

WE SQUADS

Much of the research on Millennials emphasizes their comfort and desire to collaborate with others. We are here to tell you that what you think you know is wrong! Yup, all that research, all those blog articles, all those companies selling you on developing "WE Squads" missed the mark.

A widely accepted assumption about the word *collaborate* is that Millennials like to work *in* groups to get things done. However, a fair amount of anecdotal information arising from our experiences and from interviews with Millennials indicates that this is not necessarily true. The fact is, they like to be *on* a team but still work, and be acknowledged, individually. There are slight differences between working *on* a team versus *in* a team, but they are profound and can have implications in a classroom or boardroom. Working *in* a team means that individuals are working or contributing as part of a whole, collaboratively, to achieve a common goal with dependencies and interactions on and with others. Working *on* a team means being part of a larger group working toward a common goal, but each piece is a separate responsibility.

That Millennials like to work *on* teams shouldn't be surprising since Millennials are noted as being the "trophy generation" where everyone is acknowledged for his or her effort despite the actual outcomes of the team. If we reflect on the word *team* and all it implies, we find that each individual contributes his or her part to assist the team in reaching a desired goal, and some are recognized and rewarded for individual efforts while others are not. While Millennials like to *share* their goals, desires, and interests with others, they don't always enjoy working *with* others to achieve them. The *I* in *team* has certainly emerged for this generational cohort, and the culture of competition in today's society may be one reason for such a shift in teamwork.

Sports are an oft-used metaphor for teamwork, with the reward of being tagged as the most valuable player the penultimate goal that individuals generally want to achieve. Athletes seek feedback and thrive on receiving kudos for a job well done. Even teams on the losing end of a competition give a game ball to one player who went above and beyond despite the team's loss. The competitive nature of being the *best* member of a team is what often gets an individual's adrenaline pumping and leads to a desire to win at all costs and to excel individually. We see many professional American football players punch, kick, or slam opposing players during a game to gain an edge and put others off their game when possible, all to get a win *for* the team; teams want to win while individuals seek the accolades. However, for Millennials, working in groups is perceived differently.

As a member of a group, individuals have to work with others on a regular basis with the knowledge that their individual efforts are not often recognized by those outside, or even inside, the group. In the workplace, a supervisor may need a group-effort to get a new client, but if a client declines a contract, the group is responsible for the outcome and no one gets the most valuable player (MVP) award for the loss of that contract. However, if the group is considered a team, then there is the perception that some members of the team may be blamed or lauded for the outcome. This suggests that building trust is such an important element of being a part of a group and that the group will be identified and judged as a single entity based on its collective choices. Collaboration entails an assumed trust that others are working toward common goals, but this is not always the case. Members of teams can, and often are, isolated as the scapegoat associated with a negative outcome, or equally acknowledged as the hero with a positive outcome even though the team worked together throughout the process. Think about the NFL place kicker who misses the last-second field goal that would have won the game. If this individual makes it, the team wins; if not, the player is often identified as the person responsible for the loss, even if there were fumbles, interceptions, lacks in defensive stops, or other challenges that affected the outcome of the game. Ultimately, that person has let the team down and must take the heat for the loss. This is just one example of how groups and teams are not the same. Groups require a sense of togetherness as they progress toward their end goal, all the while with the absence of individual pride. While teams seek continuity, they also require a recognition of uniqueness coupled with individual responsibility as part of that togetherness. Alas, there is an *I* in *team*; emphatically, an individual can be, and should strive to be, the MVP!

As noted in other chapters, Millennials are raised to succeed as *individuals* and are encouraged to demonstrate their individuality at all times, despite concerns from members of previous generations. There-fore, groups that are inherently perceived as collectives, wherein decisions and actions are made for the good of the group, are not as palatable for Millennials. Instead, they seek teams where they can receive individual feedback but shine as an individual and be "awarded" the MVP trophy. *Feedback* is the key term here. Millennials not only desire feedback, they demand it on an ongoing basis. This need for constant feedback is a method that Millennials use to ensure that their supervisors and co-workers know how hard they are working. The feedback loop also creates opportunities for reflection, for all involved, on whether the Millennial's performance is headed in the "right" direction. In a way, they seek out new versions of Snow-Plow Parents via supervisors and co-workers who can keep them from going down the wrong path. Sometimes, as is the case with all generations, Millennials don't always heed this advice and their performance suffers. However, sometimes they do consider the feedback but may also intentionally take additional risks that may ultimately pay off for them in the end. Where would we be if Steve Jobs or Steve Wozniak hadn't taken risks? Bill Gates? Mark Zuckerberg? Others? The Millennial risk takers are often perceived as pompous, condescending, and noncollaborative, especially when they seek advice or feedback and then don't follow it. Truthfully, many Millennials believe that they can fail or persevere on their own, as individuals. Either way, they are still viewed as "bulls in a china shop" that will take anyone or anything down along the way. Members of older generations (e.g., Baby Boomers and Gen-Xers) are well known for describing Millennials as irrational, rebellious, or chaotic in their decision-making and behaviors, especially if the outcome is unfavorable. However, since many Millennials have an entrepreneurial spirit, are often well educated, and change jobs regularly, they may wrongly perceive this risk-taking as nonthreatening. Risk is part of the equation for many Millennials who devote their finances to earning degrees that may not lead to high-paying jobs.

Additionally, social media also plays a major role in Millennials' views on collaboration. As mentioned at the beginning of this chapter, "collaboration" is about *sharing with* others, not *working with* others, and this extends to the social media lives of Millennials. Expressing concerns and accolades, seeking or providing input, and seeking out new opportunities is largely accomplished through their social networks via social media. While the brief survey that we conducted for this book indicates how reliant different generations are on family and friends for advice and support, Millennials often use social media to make these connections with those who are not present in real time, in the moment. They are more than willing to collaborate with others via social media than any other generational group and some even have social anxiety when asked to make an actual phone call. If a Gen-Xer has a pressing work or family issue, she or he might pick up the phone or private message or email colleagues, family members, or friends. However, many Millennials seek immediate gratification via Facebook, Twitter, or Instagram to garner support for their situation, thus doing so more publicly. Millennials believe that their Facebook "friends" will support their position because they have a *shared* interest in seeing that person achieve a goal. In short, many Millennials believe that *sharing* is *collaborating*. For many, having a shared interest helps them identify with others and also aids their own self-esteem and identity. To have others agree with your position, political or otherwise, simply makes you feel good, no matter how temporary.

However, one challenge with sharing your situation on social media is that many times your co-workers and employers "follow" you on social media and what you share can actually come back to haunt you.

For example, recall the communications director, Justine Sacco from a major Internet firm who tweeted "Going to Africa. Hope I don't get AIDS. Just kidding. I'm white!"[1] She made a poor social media decision, and a racist one as well. Her role as communications director in a social media world should have made her more "tech-savvy." But, her need to openly share her thoughts led to a major social media faux pas and her eventual firing after the tweet went viral. She is still suffering from the ramifications of her actions. She wanted to share her experiences in her social media world and, despite an ill-timed and insensitive tweet accompanied by an apology one day later, she may never recover her credibility. This is just one example of how the need to share with others using social media may actually hurt us in the workplace.

Do not fear. Social media collaboration can indeed lead to positive results, as is demonstrated with "grassroots" movements that begin on social media and make their way to the real world. From Occupy Wall Street to the Ukrainian and Hong Kong uprisings in 2014, collaboration can be completed successfully in a social media world. In these cases, sharing one's experiences with others can lead to worldwide support for a cause. (Re)Tweeting in favor of a grassroots movement is often seen as participating with others—and therefore *collaborating* in a Millennial sense. In these instances, sharing statuses demonstrates support for a cause and can be considered a form of cyberactivism. Millennials may not always be marching in the streets, but they lend their support for causes and movements in various other ways.

Outside of the workplace, collaboration has also evolved within educational settings as the expectations of both students and teachers have changed. As noted in other chapters, teachers, many of whom are Millennials themselves, seek collaboration with their peers not only in the lunchroom or weekly meetings, but also via social media technologies and forums or online networks, including Edmodo.[2] Edmodo is a community where teachers can share interests and connect with other teachers to discuss classroom exercises, activities, and lesson plans, among other interests. Edmodo also serves as a place for their students to submit work electronically and collaborate with each other. This tool encourages networking beyond one's own district, thus making education a truly national, even international, endeavor.

In addition to Edmodo, there are also numerous Facebook groups[3] and Twitter resources for teachers from across the nation and around the globe to share ideas and learn from each other. One such group, Grants for Teachers, provides information about available grants for classroom initiatives. Such a financial resource, merely 20 years ago, would have taken far more research and time, whereas the Internet provides immediate outlets for such collaborations.

Beyond collaborating with other educators or financers, teachers are also utilizing these online forums and networks to stay in contact with parents and students. Many parents, being technologically adept themselves, prefer to have the ability to electronically track their children's progress via a secure network and to be able to electronically connect with teachers throughout the year beyond the walls of the traditional parent–teacher conferences. This offers opportunities for parents to engage teachers on a 24/7 basis. One downside to this level of access is that teachers may become overwhelmed with communications and online expectations for being available to parents all the time. In fact, many parents expect teaches to be "on call" via social media over the weekend and throughout the night. Another, more detrimental downside to this 24/7 access is that some school districts host teachers, parents, or students from rural areas who may not, for a variety of reasons, have access to Wi-Fi or mobile Internet service or at home. Therefore, the expectation of electronic access can, and does, create a technological divide between those who have access and those who don't.

Despite this real concern, the nature of these online communities and collaborations allows Millennials to access their work at any point during the day, and also share their work with interested parents and classmates. The work submitted within these collaborative environments can also serve in building a portfolio of accomplishment whereby students can select their best work for postgraduate submissions as they progress through their schooling. Millennials' social media and electronic expectations of teachers, parents, and other students have greatly affected the ways in which education happens "after the bell rings"!

An additional concern commonly associated with social media collaboration relates to the fact that some schools have social media policies that allow for the schools or districts to use images of school-aged children in outlets of their choosing. Sometimes these images are meant to "advertise" the school's events or students' projects, but many parents may be unaware that sending a child to a certain school or school district allows for such images to be used at will for the good of the institution without considering parents' privacy concerns. Parents are sometimes shocked to find out that the elementary school their children attend are taking photos of children without consent from parents and then posting these images on the school's social media channels. One parent summed up an experience on this exact topic, which was shared by a large majority of other parents:

> As an avid user of social media in all forms, I am very conservative when it comes to my children and their use of social media. It was happenstance that I even discovered our elementary school was using images of children without parents' written consent. I was volunteering for a school party and the morning announcements were on. One announcement noted the school library now had a Twitter account. So, being the social media person that I am, I pulled out my smart phone and followed the school. What I saw shocked me—photos of elementary aged children out on the social sphere. I went straight to the principal. What upset me was that nobody asked me, a parent in the school, for my permission. I found out that the district's policy is that they don't need a parent's permission, but rather a letter opting out of taking part in social media. As you can imagine I wrote that letter immediately. However, to date, the school has not made other parents aware of this "opting out" of social media. This means photos of their children are probably floating all over the Internet without their knowledge. Beyond the fact that these images were on social media channels, personal mobile phones were used to take these pictures. This concerned me further. I don't want faculty having pictures of my children on their own mobile phones.[4]

This is a complex issue. Part of twenty-first-century learning is adapting to the changing methods of communication. However, schools need to be sure they aren't violating the rights of children.

One final, yet increasing, concern centers on the amount of collaboration students can have with each other when using social media "after the bell rings," leading to notable instances of cyberbullying. Bullying has taken place in the workplace, home, streets, and schoolyard for generations, but is now more far-reaching than ever before with the prevalence of social media and the technological savvy of Millennials and Neo-Millennials (those currently born after the Millennial group) who have grown up with technology. Although stories about hacking (a form of cyberbullying or even cyberterrorism) have been plastered throughout our media, from Home Depot and Target to Sony, it also happens on lower levels too. Many school-aged children quickly learn how to access others students' social media accounts and have also been known to create fake accounts for other students. Typically, when this occurs, the "hackers" or "bullies" create false statements or share real secrets of other students and make them public. The power of social media to spread news, accurate or not, is formidable, and many students who would have experienced in-person bullying during the school day are now being bullied 24/7 via social media. The desire to collaborate (share) with others in bringing someone "down" has clearly been amplified in this technological world.

And what about parents? How have their levels of collaboration (sharing) changed with Millennials' know-how and expectations? One clear outcome is that parents are also often on social media and contribute to the social media world. Even if someone's child is not a Facebook "friend" or Twitter follower, tech-savvy Millennials often have access to images and comments that may have once been kept more secret or private in previous generations. We can remember hearing our parents or grandparents remind us that not everything is meant for children's ears or eyes. However, we have both witnessed friends and family who post "selfies" to Instagram, Snapchat, Facebook, or Twitter where they or other adults and parents may have had a bit too much to drink or may have been in a somewhat compromising position. While it can be beneficial to be in touch with children so readily via social media, we are sure there are times when parents have thought to themselves, "I shouldn't have posted that picture" or "I shouldn't have made that drunken rant on Twitter," especially when their children may be their "friends" or "followers." We need to remember that once something is put out on social media, it lives in perpetuity. So the need to protect our children and be able to contact them in certain situations can also lead us to "share" just a bit too much with our own children when we least want to do so. Sharing is important for connecting with others but the line between private and public has certainly dwindled, if not disappeared.

However, sharing with our children is, in some instances, too important to overlook. It is the potential threat of dire circumstances in which our children (or parents) may find themselves in that potentially overrides these aforementioned awkward social media moments. Dating back to the horrible shootings at Columbine High School and the terrorism of September 11, 2001, to the shooting rampages at Virginia Tech or many U.S. malls, being able to communicate with parents, children, and law enforcement using social media has saved lives and offered peace to those involved. This type of collaboration then becomes a *need* rather than a *want* for many parents and children.

To close this discussion, Millennials have indeed put the *I* in *team* while also redefining what *collaboration* means and how it occurs. This observation is not a criticism of Millennials; rather, it serves as a reminder that with each generation, an evolution of assumed social norms and practices occurs. We are learning as we go.

7

CHARACTERISTICS 5 AND 6: COMMITTED CHANGE AGENTS

Fact or Fiction: Millennials lack self-motivation and their laziness is a detriment to change.

TURN AND FACE THE CHANGE, NO MATTER HOW STRANGE

Many Millennials exhibit a progressive attitude toward entrepreneurial, philanthropic, political, workplace, environmental, and diversity-focused ideals that are left over from prior generations. While not all Millennials should be considered change agents, there are those who tend to set the bar high for others around them. Many may indeed be surprised by the lengths to which some Millennials will go to make change happen.

We have all encountered individuals who lack motivation, expertise, or basic ability to institute or lead change. However, we are certain that each of us has also interacted with people who are motivated by internal and external desires and that are capable and competent change agents. In this sense, Millennials are no different. Yes, some Millennials feel entitled, seek acknowledgment and satisfaction from others, and are simply not interested in leading. But many Millennials actively seek to promote change in a number of areas including human rights, political activism, and technology or other cutting-edge fields.

BUSINESS

The notion of going to work and waiting until you have established yourself in your career before accomplishing great things is almost passé. If Elizabeth Holmes, Bill Gates, Mark Zuckerberg, Abigail Johnson, and others had waited that long, where would they be today?[1] What we see is that many Millennials actively seek challenges, and, in doing so, strike out on their own by starting a business, often without a college degree. However, since education is so highly valued among this generation, many do earn degrees, get jobs, and then seek and pursue change once they are a part of the workforce. We note that Millennials appear to be much more willing to move to other companies to seek new challenges or advancement opportunities within their careers. As a result, they may not hold the same level of company loyalty held by previous generations, especially Traditionalists and Baby Boomers. With such an adventurist and entrepreneurial spirit, Millennials seek change rather than wait for it; they are active participants, not passive, in defining their career paths. This is one of the reasons that Millennials seek so much feedback from their peers or managers. Let's take a closer look at this industrial personality.

ENTREPRENEURIAL SPIRITS ARISE

What is clear is that many Millennials are in the driver's seat when it comes to developing their own startups, whether for-profit or not. One such example is that of twenty-four-year-old David Burstein, author of *Fast Future: How the Millennial Generation Is Shaping Our World*. He explains how he and some of his high school classmates seized the opportunity to turn their passion for film into a much larger endeavor—an entire film festival. Specifically, in 2004 David and his friends created a film festival open only to high school students. Over a period of seven months, these Millennials launched the inaugural Westport Youth Film Festival with support from a local movie theater for showing the films, and the film festival is now in its tenth year. This initial passion for creating change grew into a more focused passion for the political process and voting. David's passion for Millennials and what they bring to the world is conveyed in his book and he refers to Millennials as being pioneers of "The Next Big Thing."[2]

Let's also take a look at another Millennial on the rise, Elizabeth Holmes. Many of us may not be familiar with her; yet she is the only female billionaire to crack the top ten who wasn't born into a household name like Mars (Candy Company), Walton (Walmart), or Jobs (Steve Jobs's widow). She has created her own path to success. Much like Harvard dropout Mark Zuckerberg, she is a Stanford engineering dropout who found her entrepreneurial spirit in the health industry. Holmes formed Theranos, a healthcare solutions company with the vision of bringing health information accessibility to everyone, at the young age of nineteen. Her company offers spa-like, relaxing atmospheres for microsample lab testing that encourages people to take charge of their health at a low cost. The company has created wellness centers in Palo Alto, California, and throughout Arizona with expansion plans in the works all over the country through an established partnership with Walgreens.[3] As of October 2014, Theranos is valued at over $9 billion—not bad for a thirty year old. Her drive and vision may indeed lead to greater change and expectations for health care in the United States and beyond.

These are only two examples of countless Millennial shining stars who are determined to make their own way. Each had the support of others and a vision to make things happen. So much can be learned from these Millennials and clearly defy the oft-held opinion that Millennials are lazy or lack self-motivation. However, it would be irresponsible for us to propose that all Millennials have this same drive or vision. What we can propose is that, whether we like it or not, Millennials are change agents through intention or happenstance and we must dig a bit deeper to understand these changes. Since a key word in this chapter is *agent,* we will take a moment and focus on how Millennials take an active role in changing the expectations in the workplace, the classroom, and at home.

WORKPLACE DEMANDS

In addition to promoting an entrepreneurial spirit, many Millennials are making workplace demands that are influencing how businesses conduct their daily affairs. We know that Millennials are contributing to the evolution of the traditional workplace expectations and schedule, and we recognize just how flexible they perceive everyone to be. We also hear them "toot their own horn" about how technologically savvy they are. Each generation brings change over time, yet this generation expects it to happen quickly and, they believe, more efficiently. Let's begin this conversation by focusing on the workday schedules for a moment.

With the advent of computers, the Internet, smartphones, and social media, many Millennials believe that they can, and should, be allowed to work on their own timetable. Many are willing to be on call 24/7, as long as they don't have to physically be at work in the early morning hours. Millennials should not be characterized as "the lazy folks" that they are often pegged to be. Rather, they prefer to have a certain degree of flexibility in how and when the work gets done. If they can work flexible schedules, say from 11:00 a.m. to 7:00 p.m., and be "on" during all other hours, they would gladly prefer to be able to work those hours. Many can, and do, like early hours, but the key here is flexibility. As we have learned, many Millennials sleep with their phones beside them at night, often checking emails, texts, and social media sites, even while in a dream state. This means the typical night of sleep is severely reduced for Millennials and many struggle to be active and coherent in the early morning hours. (This trend is also seen with many Gen-Xers and late Baby Boomers.) Many Millennials choose to live their connected lives to the fullest due to their need to know what is happening at all times. As work practices evolve, many companies are becoming aware that a lot of work can be completed "after hours" and are beginning to reward these employees by paying for their computer and smartphone services. This evolution will continue to promote the idea that Millennials will need to further adapt to an increasingly flexible work schedule to maintain their work–life balance.

Additionally, Millennials' continued online presence also sets an increased expectation that co-workers, supervisors, teachers, parents, CEOs, and others should also be available online at all hours. What this means is that when they post a comment, question, or status update at 2:00 in the morning, they may believe that you "should" be providing an *immediate* response. While Millennials know that this is not truly realistic, there is a minority who may indeed expect this *immediate* response.

Expectations such as this have led to some companies hiring salaried employees whose role is to *troll* or scan the Internet and email systems to gauge the pulse of their workers and consumer base at all hours. For example, there are some government employees who "hang out," or troll, certain sites to teach, even guide, the perceptions on topics ranging from legal matters to financial, political, and personal matters. In a corporate setting, simply following standard ethical guidance should curb trolling for deceptive or manipulative reasons. However, companies do, and often very effectively, troll all varieties of online media to gain an edge or even assist in managing a crisis more effectively. Roles within companies that are responsible for this type of surveillance require a need for a new position called "social media specialist";[4] these employees are hired to blog; respond on behalf of a CEO or company; keep Facebook interesting; capture or create videos for YouTube; snap photos for Instagram; hold Twitter chats about policies, products, or services; or learn more about the clientele and employees. In other words, social media specialists are paid to address employee concerns at any point during the course of a day, including weekends, when those who would normally answer may indeed be away. These employees are asked to interact with consumers and other company officials as needed and over a variety of social media outlets. What this suggests is that companies no longer leave an answering machine on overnight and pick up messages in the morning. It also shows that the workday doesn't begin at 9:00 a.m. and end at 5:00 p.m. anymore. This expectation of "reach" has changed the workday for customers, employees, and employers alike. Companies must account for these extra demands put on their workforce, especially outside of what were once identified as "traditional" working hours.

DIVERSITY AND CHANGING DEMOGRAPHICS

In addition to being technologically savvy and extremely interactive in their online worlds, many Millennials are also accustomed to a more diverse workforce in ways that far surpass their generational predecessors. Millennials were born largely to late Baby Boomers and early Gen-Xers who, as mentioned in chapter 1, may have embraced civil, women's, and LGBTQ rights on a national and international level. This basis of beliefs and equality has had an effect on their children, who subsequently account for a majority of the Millennials who are currently in the workplace. Millennials see an increased need for organizations to embrace globalization in order to be successful and account for the changing demographics as well. This suggests that Millennials have a much lower tolerance for workplace discrimination in all of its forms, from gender pay inequity to bias against those with disabilities or differing gender and sexual identities. Millennials continue to witness large numbers of immigrants living, studying, and possibly struggling (legally or illegally); engage in increased study abroad or international volunteer opportunities,[5, 6] and provide services to many local, regional, or national groups or organizations as part of a service learning programs.[7, 8] The latter example sets the tone for an ethic of care that many Millennials embrace.

CHANGING EDUCATIONAL VISION: FORGET COMMON CORE. LET'S TALK SERVICE AND SOCIAL MEDIA!

As highlighted in previous chapters, many teachers were trained to be the *sage on the stage* as it relates to traditional educational models. Students would come to class, take notes, regurgitate the information that the teacher provided, and sit quietly with little to no interaction. Ask anyone from the Silent Generation (Traditionalists) or Baby Boomer Generation, and this description of the classroom rings true. As Gen-Xers were progressing through their school years, teachers were simply trained to teach in a way that was far removed from such a banking concept of teaching toward a more engaged audience. A great example of actively seeking ways to empower students in their learning rather than sitting back and banking the information for the sole benefit of the teacher is to allow students to play a more active part in the learning process, which is much preferred over a passive one.[9]

This approach doesn't imply that teachers are not to be respected or that what they teach is no longer valuable. Instead, teachers can use their knowledge to empower students to take an active role in the learning process. The evolution of the classroom continues today in many schools, including Montessori and charter schools, in ways never imagined as a result of the introduction of technology, specifically computers. Many of us can recall the time in our schooling when computers were first introduced. If we fast-forward to today's schools and the schools of the Millennials, we can see that students are often required, where possible, to complete written homework on computers, conduct Internet research, use apps, create Prezi or PowerPoint presentations, and play educational games, among other tasks, on a daily basis. Although a digital divide still exists in many areas, students can typically gain access to computers during and after school and at public libraries. Computers have become an assumed basic, much like a calculator.

Nowadays, students aren't only expected to be connected technologically, they are also expected to be connected geographically. This means that students are more frequently volunteering in their communities (colleges even ask for a running list on their applications), and are being asked to engage in various levels of service learning. In these situations, students learn in both the classroom and at home, and are required to take part in some type of preorganized event within the community. For example, students taking media literacy may have a service learning component where they visit after-school programs or classes to discuss the media representation of diversity, privacy, and media effects. Even students in an accounting class may be asked to offer free basic tax service to members of the local community. Since many Millennial students have already volunteered with various service organizations as part of their education, they often embrace these service learning components as a way to see how their lessons can be applied in the real world. In fact, often when researching job opportunities, students will seek out organizations that give back to the community in some way, such as organized walks or fundraisers for local charities. Those Millennials who engage in these types of service projects and seek these career opportunities may often become the next leaders within their communities.

In addition to service, Millennials are also demanding that their teachers use instructional strategies that engage them where they are: in a fast-paced, technological world. Students want to have access to their teachers after class and even on weekends, and some teachers see this as an opportunity to keep the learning process moving. Many college students now expect that teachers will include some social media component during class, whether it's a Twitter feed or a blog post on WordPress. Students want to be able to use their voices more regularly both inside and outside of the classroom. While email may have been the great connector in the early 2000s, texting, Twitter, and Facebook (along with other social media channels) are where connections and conversations are happening now. More than half of students from ages twelve through seventeen have smartphones,[10] and they expect to text and receive texts all of the time, even during class; it's like an itch they must scratch. So are there ways for teachers to acknowledge this itch and to incorporate smartphones and technology in productive and educational ways? Absolutely.

Outside of class, for example, some instructors have adopted the use of Twitter chats for exam preparation, incorporated blogs for initiating student-led class discussions, and initiated RSS feeds to encourage students to read the most up-to-date news from organizations of interest. These same instructors have also used private Pinterest groups to provide supplemental information for the class, Facebook and Twitter to generate outreach after class, and WordPress to have students post research and guide discussions. Within the classroom, an increasing number of instructors are engaging in a type of teaching known as the *flipped classroom*[11] (mentioned earlier in the book), where students complete knowledge-based tasks using various social media, reading, research, and gaming tools. Activities from the flipped classroom are often completed at home with the students returning to class ready to apply the materials during a different classroom activity. These activities engage the student and can often lead to the identification of potential weaknesses that a student may exhibit. Some teachers also use Twitter feeds during class for students to pose questions about course materials and then reserve time near the end of class to address those discussions. Clearly, there are ways to meet the technological needs of students without compromising the integrity of the classroom and the respect for what teachers bring to the classroom environment.

ENGAGING THE POLITICAL MACHINE

For a number of years, many late Baby Boomers and early Gen-Xers showed little interest in government and politics. Phrases like "Don't Trust Anyone Over 30" and "Power to the People" became popular during the 1960s and empowered citizens to voice their opinions and views in public arenas.[12] The 1960s were a tumultuous time of change and many people were interested in changing the way that the United States engaged *all* of its citizens and the decision-making process related to war (or police actions). Uprisings were a deep expression of the general distrust and frustrations that many Gen-Xers had toward their government during that time, with a leak of classified information in the Pentagon Papers[13] and the Watergate scandal[14] not helping matters either. This distrust settled a bit in the late 1970s, 1980s, and early 1990s, but has been reemerging and gaining support with Millennials.

After years of presidential mishaps, from sexual scandals to "weapons of mass destruction" inaccuracies, Millennials emerged as a formidable force in the 2008 presidential election. It may be easier to see now in retrospect, but if we look at the tension that existed between the campaigns of then-Senator Barack Obama and the elder Senator John McCain, and couple that with the growing capacity of the Internet and birth of social media, we can begin to see the influence that Millennials had on this important political moment in our history.

Senator Barack Obama had only been making waves in Illinois for a short time in the early 2000s. Young voters, many of whom were Millennials, became enamored with him, not only a successful black man, but also a forthright politician who could read the pulse of young voters. Millennials rallied around him and almost dared him to run for office in 2008. History, of course, tells us that he accepted this challenge. Young voters were enthusiastically engaged in his message of *Change* and his campaign manager fueled this fire using social media. This was the first time in the nation's history that social media were prominently and effectively incorporated to gain power and presence in a political campaign.[15] Not only did Millennials rally online, but they also attended and organized many pro-Obama campaigns. All of this was happening while John McCain was executing a fairly "traditional" campaign; his campaign was missing a key generational group that was eagerly awaiting a chance to promote change. A platform centered on change was just what Millennials were seeking and Barack Obama became president-elect in 2008. We know that things continued to evolve in the political arena as social media grew in popularity between 2008 and 2012 and included a growing Twitter presence for Obama's reelection. At this point, the expectation was that politicians would have to engage young voters over a variety of social media platforms to earn their vote, and their respect. While both Republicans and Democrats alike engaged in social media direct messaging by pushing their messages out, perceived dialogue with young voters was more pertinent than actual dialogue, as "digital technology allows leaders to engage in a new level of 'conversation' with voters, transforming campaigning into something more dynamic, more of a dialogue, than it was in the 20th century."[16]

Another example of how Millennials are taking control of their political interests is how they engage in different types of activism. Before the introduction of social media and the Internet, activism involved groups of people attending a civic march, rally, parade, or protest in person with a clear threat of being arrested by police if your actions crossed the line. The threat of arrest is still very real as was seen in the Ferguson, Missouri, protests following a shooting that involved police officer Darren Wilson and young, black, male teenager Michael Brown. Citizens from near and far took to the streets to protest the shooting—and many were arrested for doing so. While these types of protests can potentially cross legal boundaries, others can lead to change and increased awareness, such as Take Back the Night rallies. One example of promoting change is the Occupy Movement.[17] While this movement was not the brainchild of Millennials, many Millennials took to local parks all across the world to stage their protests regarding social and political inequalities. This rallying cry soon grew into a specific protest against the bailout of Wall Street and big business, but then morphed into larger movements focused on other topics including housing, unemployment, and student loans, among other issues. While the Occupy Movement has not been the focus of media attention today, many events still take place. How do people know about these events and this organization: social media? With the prominence of Twitter, people need only to search the hashtag (the pound sign #) on Twitter.com (#OCCUPYTOGETHER) to keep abreast of trending topics and events.

With this information in hand, the importance of an effective hashtag can't be overlooked. Since many Millennials and, seemingly, just as many of their Gen-Xer counterparts, don't prefer to engage in in-person activism, hashtag activism is a new route to gain a following, increase awareness, and implement change. While many media and social critics claim that hashtag activism is a lazy, uninvolved form of involvement, these events and hashtags certainly garner much media criticism.

The idea of a "digital grassroots" movement actually reaches people where they are most active and is an effective way to garner attention for ideas—from the ground up, grassroots style. Take the 2013 amyotrophic lateral sclerosis (ALS) Ice Bucket Challenge as an example. Here is a nonprofit organization that seeks donations for research in fighting this disease. While their donation streams are consistent, one large shift in their level of donations began with a single challenge to dump an ice bucket of water over one's head or donate $100 to ALS. This went viral. Although the initial connection between the ice bucket and ALS was not intentional, it took on a digital life of its own as it spread on Facebook and onto Twitter. This soon became a nomination-focused request on Facebook and Twitter with the #icebucketchallenge hashtag. As of October 24, 2014, the initiative had raised $115 million, which far surpasses the organization's prior year's revenues, which were listed at $29 million for 2013.[18] The fact is, people from every generation took part in this challenge and usually completed the challenge *and* donated. If this type of initiative is considered non-grassroots, lazy, or unmotivated, then perhaps we should reconsider the definition of activism to include viral video power that raises awareness.

Millennials are also turning to technology in times of uncertainty throughout the world to document their struggles. Citizens caught in the middle of international conflicts, including the uprisings in the Ukraine and Hong Kong, turned to Twitter and Instagram to capture their protests and promote their social movements in 2013 and 2014, respectively. In the Ukraine, protestors gathered in Independence Square in Kiev to protest proposed allied connections to Russia in lieu of stronger European connections. The Social Media and Political Participation Lab at New York University noted just how early in the protests that social media was playing a role: "Our findings suggest that social media, as it has throughout these protests, continues to be a pivotal organization tool for those in Kiev and also the most relevant mechanism for disseminating and exchanging information both within Ukraine and abroad."[19] An increasing number of protestors continue to share photos, tweets, and Facebook posts about their experiences, often becoming "i-reporters" of the event in action. Social media are still playing a role in this conflict and Millennials are predominant drivers of its utilization and adoption.

A similar social media presence was experienced during the Hong Kong protests in the fall of 2014. Students have been pressing for bi-governmental structures, often classed "One Country, Two Systems" for decades, with China allowing Hong King to run its own elections and have a nominal level of democracy. While photographs captured much of the student protests during this time, including one memorable moment of a student facing tanks in the streets during the Tiananmen Square protests of 1989,[20] students today turned to the Chinese version of Twitter, Weibo, and other social media, including Instagram and Facebook, to promote change. Regardless, in today's world, any protest, rally, march, event, or moment can be captured and relayed across various media platforms. Once they "go viral" or "trend," momentum builds and results are promising.

AN ETHIC OF CARE LEADS THE WAY FOR MANY MILLENNIALS

Millennials want to be heard and often seek out the most efficient avenues for conveying their message. Not only do they want to have their voices heard, but they also want their acts of kindness to be embraced and recognized. While some Millennials are indeed selfish and unmotivated, many are just the opposite and are actually selfless and motivated for the betterment of others.

Some Millennials identify opportunities within organizations that focus on the betterment of the greater good. While they enjoy making money, Millennials also desire to get more out of an organization; therefore, they often want to take part in an event, support a cause, or donate money. Whether fighting illiteracy or homelessness, supporting the American Society for the Prevention of Cruelty to Animals, or promoting equality throughout the world, many Millennials have kind hearts and want to help those they view as less fortunate or oppressed. Despite the bad economic times and heavy unemployment among this generation, many Millennials still have a positive outlook on their future and the futures of others. In an Achieve survey of just over 1,500 Millennials, 47 percent had volunteered in a nonprofit the previous year while 87 percent had donated money to a cause of their liking.[21] In a blog post from June 23, 2014, the author notes that the "*2014 Millennial*

Impact Report showed that a company's involvement with cause-related opportunities influenced all stages of development—from a Millennial's decision whether or not to accept a job (more than 55 percent said they were persuaded to say yes after 'cause' work was discussed during an interview), to whether or not they planned to stay at a job."[22] Employers may be best served by supporting the Millennials' drive to take part in helping others and by supporting specific causes as part of their own company mission. In addition, Millennials often seek out organizations that are known to support a cause when searching for jobs or internships. Let's take a quick look at some of the philanthropic ventures that Millennials have taken part in or control of over the past few years.

MILLENNIAL PHILANTHROPY: NOT A LOST CAUSE

In addition to entrepreneurs like David Burstein and Elizabeth Holmes and big-name philanthropists like Bill and Melinda Gates, there are many lesser known and less financially well-off Millennials creating their own nonprofits out of an ethic of care, not solely an economic drive.

We will start with a late-twenty-something named Kyle Smitley, who is the founder of Detroit Achievement Academy and owner and creator of a carbon-neutral, organic children's clothing line called Barley & Birch.[23] Educated at Depauw University, Kyle created the company during her first year as a law student. She used her undergraduate majors in geology and philosophy and her minors in Spanish and chemistry to found this multimillion-dollar company. However, after a few years of hanging with big wigs like Warren Buffet, Kyle realized that there was something missing from her life. Although her company had donated to many not-for-profit organizations around the world, Kyle had a yearning for something more. Leveraging her prior experiences with her desire to give to others inspired her to found a charter school in Detroit. It became widely known that she was supporting education on many fronts and soon Ellen Degeneres, host of TV's *Ellen,* invited Kyle on her show to tell her story. Snapchat even gave an additional $25,000 to support her initiative. In this case, Kyle's millions couldn't make her happy and instead she used her passion for something different, guided by an ethic of care, to do something worthwhile in a community in much need of help.

Another philanthropic Millennial is G. Ryan Ansin, a social entrepreneur, who began his philanthropic work when he was twelve, and continues that work today. Ryan started a nonprofit called "Every Person Has A Story" (EPHAS) where he and others visit people all around the world and teach them how to use cameras so that they can tell their own stories rather than have photographers tell those stories for them. These stories are told for the bettering of the community, not for entertainment purposes.[24] The company has thirty-two locations in twelve countries and now allows others to use the set-up to continue its work.[25] While the success of EPHAS has been demonstrated, Ryan has now moved on to other projects including the Clarity Project.[26] Here again we see a Millennial take charge of his own destiny, commit to causes he believes in, and create new organizations. Clearly these two Millennials have more drive than many, but their interest in helping others and creating that space for themselves is exemplary, even invigorating, as role models for the Me Generation.

Not only are Millennials starting their own successful service-based organizations, but this generation has also redefined philanthropy and giving as it is traditionally defined. Prior to the advent of the Internet and social media, fundraising was often done in person, at special events, or via postal service mailings. The online world has now grown as an effective outlet to increase charitable giving. While typical online donations hover around 15 percent (excluding the extremely successful ALS Challenge mentioned previously), this method of philanthropy is growing each year. More importantly, many Millennials not only want to take part in charitable events, but they also want to tell the world that they were involved in the cause using social media sites like Instagram, Facebook, Flickr, and others. Millennials demonstrate continued loyalty to organizations that they engage with charitable contributions and are extremely passionate for certain causes.[27]

Beyond meeting Millennials in their technologically engaged environment, Millennials are also changing the very definition of *philanthropy*. The traditional definition has shifted from "Love of humankind in the form of time, talent and treasure" to include *voice* and *network* such that advocating for a cause and educating others as well as using personal and professional relational networks to benefit a cause are now important components of the definition.[28] But Millennials want to be kept in the financial loop of the organization. Knowing where and how money is being spent and also which services and programs are successful is very important to them.[29] In other words, organizations are being asked to be more accountable for the funds they raise and programs and services they offer if they want to continue to reach Millennials, and their wallets!

So, with their commitment, Millennials certainly can lead change in the United States and elsewhere. As parents, teachers, co-workers, and employers, we would be best served by these types of Millennials if we engage their interests and participate for change. The time is now for each generation to continue on its own path and become, or continue to be, committed change agents. Change is a process that is ongoing and much change is still needed in our world today. Seems like these two "Cs" are worthwhile for us all.

8

CHARACTERISTIC 7: CONTRADISTINCTIVE

Fact or Fiction: Millennials are contradistinctive.

GET REAL! NO TWO GENERATIONS ARE COMPLETELY OPPOSITE

Take a moment to think back to when you were younger. Did you ever want to be just like your parents? Your grandparents? Your friends? Chances are that most of us generally pledged to be different from our parents or grandparents, especially once we entered middle school. In fact, we refer to those years as the *preteen* and *teen years,* and during those years it is expected that we will rebel against those we perceive as trying to control us. Ironically, this often includes our teachers, parents, and work supervisors. As teens and young adults, we don't ask them to tell us what to do or how to do it; rather, we "know" what we want and how to get there. Therefore, we typically identify more closely with people who are closer in age because we perceived them as being more like "us." Often, these are the people with whom we get into trouble. During this age, we may be sent to our rooms for "talking back," or sent to the principal's office for "being rude" or "disruptive," or even fired from a job because we "stood up" for our beliefs. Those moments of glory that we experience before the punishment enable some of us to recognize that the end results aren't always worth it, while others are empowered by those actions and don't mind the consequences.

For example, when Baby Boomers were growing up, many were sent to Catholic schools and regale us with stories about the nuns using their rulers to smack or use a paddle on students who were perceived to be unruly or disrespectful. In turn, many of those Baby Boomers may themselves have used an equally forceful method of discipline with their own children, and yet will take a stand against the school systems and their chosen methods of discipline. Like their Baby Boomer or Traditionalist parents, many Gen-Xers have also experienced stiff punishment in the home. Some choose to dismiss those methods in raising their children while others embrace the values set forth from their youth and model their discipline methods after their parents. This is just one example of how generations can never really be considered contradistinctive (complete opposites). It is, however, important to keep in mind that some discipline styles are deeply rooted in particular areas of the United States, and are about larger cultural traditions specific to that society (i.e., race, class, and sex factors). In fact, while many people are against a heightened level of discipline in school systems and punishment methods have been debated nationwide, there is currently no federal prohibition.[1] A recent example garnering headlines occurred in 2014 and included an NFL football player who took to using a switch to discipline his then four-year-old son. He was suspended from his job and had a prolonged legal battle resulting from his actions;[2] the debate surrounding this issue centered on cultural upbringing versus assault of a child. What was clear was that this older Millennial was similarly punished as a child. In this case he was not as much contradistinctive as openly similar in his actions. So we ask, just how contradistinctive are Millennials from other generations, *really*? While Millennials tend to be contradistinctive in some actions, there are also key areas where the similarities to previous generations are quite similar, especially at different points in their lifetime. This may indicate that, in many ways, history does indeed repeat itself when we examine "various times in our lives."[3]

Millennials are often described as a unique generation. What seems more likely, though, is that they are not complete opposites from their generational predecessors. In fact, Millennials have noted differences based on historical context, their opportunities, and current events that influence how they perceive the world. This means that while life circumstances may have changed from generation to generation, the successes and struggles that each age group experiences during their lives (e.g., college graduates or teens) are quite similar. It is obvious that we resemble each other in many basic ways, despite generational differences, especially when looking at educational and workplace contexts.

One such similarity between generations can be seen in their approaches to harmony and peace and standing up for their beliefs. Although generational views on definitions of what is considered right and wrong may be different, each generation's heart is in the right place. Let's take perceptions of war and politics as an example. While Baby Boomers may have felt the need for unity and peace after World War II, many later Baby Boomers and early Gen-Xers demanded world peace and justice in the United States. Demonstrations related to these movements took place via protests, both peaceful and violent.

Governance and policies on civil rights also exemplify how experiences shape generational differences. Following World War II, law enforcement often took decisions into their own hands, resulting in violence against unarmed or unconfirmed armed protestors. We only have to look at Selma, Alabama, in 1965[4] and the Kent State incident in 1970[5] to see prime examples of such behaviors. Even as we write this book, there are racially charged incidents present in our media, including blatant hate crimes, such as Millennial Dylann Storm Roof's massacre of nine people in Charleston, South Carolina, on June 17, 2015. During the late 1950s and early 1960s, clashes between later Silent Generation (Traditionalists)/early Baby Boomers with Later Baby Boomers/early Gen-Xers were prevalent. Changes in civil rights and, later, gay rights closely resembled each other as potential progress was often thwarted by contemporary beliefs, policies, norms, and rules. There isn't a single generation that escapes the confrontations and conflicts that lead to change. However, technological advancements throughout each generation can, and do, change the way these events unfold and technology is one way in which generations can indeed be contradistinctive. Let's look at ways in which Millennials can, and do, challenge each other and other generations, and also the ways in which Millennials are, at times, contradistinctive.

CONNECTEDNESS

As previously discussed in the chapter on Millennial connectivity, this generation lives in a world where being "on" 24/7 is becoming an expectation, not an anomaly. They often sleep with their cell phones next to their beds, sometimes sleep-text (answer a text while not fully awake), and often check their phones throughout the night. Some even resort to the "Texts From Last Night" site that allows them to review what they have missed while asleep. Fear of missing out (FOMO) plays a large part in the anxiety and stress many Millennials feel, which also suggests that being so connected can be detrimental. One example of FOMO occurs in a classroom exercise for a Media Literacy course. Here, the professor asks her students to avoid electronic texting and online communication for a period of 24 hours. "Oh, the horror!" Many students begin to ask why they even have to complete this assignment. They know they are "hooked," but so what, "It's expected!" Many dread the consecutive hours without that contact while some strategically plan their day "away." They report that their friends and family express deep concern over that person's "silence" even when told ahead of time about the assignment. What this exercise also reveals is that many students find that the time that they are disconnected is rather peaceful and fruitful, and they actually accomplish quite a bit. But it also reveals that those same students, and others who despise the mandatory moratorium required for class, won't go "tech-free" after the assignment is completed even when they experience the benefits. Most cite FOMO as their primary reason, while many are working at jobs where social media is a mandatory part of the gig and not simply a leisurely activity. From retail sales to pizza delivery, the world has gone "techno-crazy" and "being on" is about being connected. This is truly one way in which Millennials are contradistinctive from other generations. While others may be embedded in this technological renaissance now, Millennials have always been integrated with technology, and the Neo-Millennials who follow will be even more embedded.

This feeling of being connected ties directly to the "Culture of Personality," which is most often seen in Millennials today and which may also render Millennials more contradistinctive.[6] In this type of culture, those who are more socially dynamic and present (we suggest virtual presence counts too!) receive the most attention, and, as we know,

Millennials have been raised to be the focus of attention; just note the number of selfies they post to Twitter, Instagram, and Facebook. If they can't be at the center of attention at home, at school, or in the workplace, then many Millennials use social media to brand themselves and electronically acquire more followers, friends, likes, or comments to promote that attention. This stands in stark contrast to many Gen-Xers and Baby Boomers who are social media literate but who also don't understand the need to update their status in ways that have previously been deemed "awkward." For example, sharing one's drunken stupor on Facebook or Instagramming your baby's ultrasound or even verbally bullying others on Twitter, Facebook, or Yik Yak is incomprehensible to many Silent Generation members and Baby Boomers; yet many Millennials and late Gen-Xers deem these acceptable codes of conduct. In a 24/7 world where personal and private are now often indistinguishable, these moments of perceived social ineptness and inappropriateness often go unfiltered and can lead to lawsuits, loss of jobs, divorce, and other consequences. One example is a former Major League Baseball player who, in 2015, tweeted his daughter's acceptance to college and then had to personally and legally pursue some people on the Twitterverse for their distasteful and abusive posts about his daughter.[7] Some of the people sending the repulsive tweets were fired from their jobs, while others are being sued for their tweets. These people now know firsthand how social media activity, when unfiltered, can lead to dire consequences, and they are not alone.

Since we live in this "Culture of Personality," perhaps we should laud the notion that we need to shift back to its predecessor, the calm, cool, and collected "Culture of Character" instead.[8] In a "Culture of Character," the focus is on one's internal thoughts and beliefs where who you are as a person is determined by the control exhibited and the morality attached to actions; thoughtfulness and listening are deemed priorities. This culture, unfortunately, has taken a backseat to the "Culture of Personality" where being "on" and publicly present is par for the course. Celebrities, paparazzi, trending tweets, and viral videos make being in the limelight a cultural norm, if not an expectation. The fine line between our personal and private lives is dwindling as babies' photos are plastered on the Internet via social media so their lives are public from birth (sometimes even before). This may indeed be one way in which Millennials and future generations are contradistinctive, while another is the way in which friends and friendships are defined.

DEFINING *FRIENDS*

Despite the fact that computer-mediated opportunities existed prior to the late 1990s and early 2000s, it wasn't until computers became readily affordable and user-friendly, much like televisions in the 1950s and cell phones in the late 1980s, that they entered homes and provided opportunities for an extended network of connectivity. Now it is likely that despite financial divides present in U.S. culture and elsewhere, a large majority of people have access to the Internet either in their own homes or hands, and seek connectivity 24/7. If they don't, most local libraries offer that amenity for free, and Wi-Fi has become an expectation everywhere we go. With at-home and on-the-go computer access, the prevalence of social media was born. In the early 1990s, virtual communities were connected via listservs (many still exist today) and email provided a quick connection to others. Then a new millennium arrived and rapid changes in connectivity changed how friendships were created, sustained, and ended.

In 2003, MySpace was introduced to the media world and so began the first truly accessible, user-friendly social medium available from the home. MySpace also became one of the key places where young Millennials expressed themselves early and often, while also requesting or earning a following. Fast-forward ten years, and we now see many more competing options for self-expression and social connectivity. Facebook overpowered MySpace in the mid-2000s until it ostensibly made it disappear or at least become irrelevant. As trends change, Facebook is also slowly losing users as newer social media engage privacy concerns and offer similar services with less advertising (for now), such as Oovoo. However, what is clear is that one of the goals of any social medium (e.g., Instagram, Facebook, Twitter) is to engage people so that they wish to become a "friend" or "follower." Facebook users and Tweeters (among others) hope to "trend" and YouTube video creators hope to have their videos "go viral." The idea of reaching out to friends, family, and other users (strangers) has become an important focus for many Millennials. Silent Generation members usually made friends in person and within their physical proximity, and unless they traveled or were in the military, they generally didn't make friends afar. Even having pen pals meant that someone had a direct, firsthand connection to and knowledge of someone living in a distant location. Enter the Baby Boomers who had increasing access to television, a better U.S. infrastructure to travel, and the postwar money to do so. They were often more financially capable of moving away from the areas in which they grew up to move to the suburbs, other states, or different countries. However, the Baby Boomers' friends were still considered those people with whom they had regular in-person interaction. If we now look at the late Gen-Xers and the advent of the cell phone, and ultimately the Internet in mobile form, things haven't been quite the same. Many early Gen-Xers believed and still believe in the interpersonal relationships developed by in-person interactions, but as chat rooms and other online communities emerged, some of those early Gen-Xers and their late Gen-Xer counterparts began to connect with people from all over the world. This computer-mediated relational development has continued to change who we "reach" and who we consider "friends" in our lives today. Now consider Millennials who grew up in this world and who may have been Skyping since birth (mostly later Millennials and post-Millennials). Friendship is still important but the ways in which they are developed are drastically different.

As Gen-Xers on different ends of the timeline, we can recall how friends were usually those with whom we had regular contact on a frequent basis. Often based on extracurricular or curricular activities, friends were those with similar likes, dislikes, tastes, and other social factors (e.g., geography, class, religion). Friends were often neighbors who engaged in fun outdoor games like kick the can, hide and seek, stickball or other recreational activities. Nowadays, however, children, who have often been overprotected and overscheduled, may find that their friends are no longer within close physical proximity. Instead, they can be accessed via email, text, instant message, Facebook, Skype, or Twitter, and can even be on opposite ends of the world where they met via online gaming or interacting in a specialized chat room. Physical proximity is often replaced with virtual proximity based on interests. One important caveat is that some Millennials who grow up with fewer educational, cultural, or extracurricular experiences because of their parents' financial, religious, or geographic situations may indeed rely

more on physical proximity for friendship building than their generational counterparts. In many cases, cell phones are quickly replacing
landlines in many of these homes and smartphones are often considered necessities, not desires, except in very rural or poverty-stricken
areas. Therefore, children may have access to and seek friends from
outside their neighborhood.

Millennials also rely on their friends, no matter how they are defined, for support and advice, and therefore will often make decisions
using feedback from their friends on social media. Social media provides an outlet to raise questions about the best plumber or worst restaurant in an area, but can also be a place where close friends can be
privately messaged or Skyped (videochat) for more personal advice.
When we look at the results from a small survey that was conducted for
this book, we found that no matter how limited, Millennials tend to rely
more on their parents for advice about everything from a bad breakup
to possible career changes to financial matters. Parents, in a sense, have
been considered friends by many Millennials, thus lessening the generational divide between parent and child in that relationship. We also
noted that many times when a life partner was in the picture, many of
these matters were kept between these two parties, thus in a way mod-
ifying, if not ending, the previously established parental friendship. Because of these parent–child friendships and how they are publicly dis-
played, those looking in from the outside of that relationship may perceive children as disrespectful. This perceived disrespect of one's parents sometimes carries over into Millennials' educational experiences,
when teachers, who are often their parents' ages, spend the day with
them in the classroom.

PROBLEMS AND OPPORTUNITIES ARISE WITH FRIENDS

At this point, it should not come as a surprise that relationships within
the classroom have also evolved over time. Most Baby Boomers and
Gen-Xers interacted with instructors, teachers, and mentors with different expectations. In many classrooms prior to the advent of social media, teachers were often considered "alien" to their students. In fact,
seeing one's teacher in the supermarket or restroom left many students
in a conundrum: How can their teachers be *like* them? Prior to the

1990s, most teachers garnered parent-like respect because the title of *educator* carried a certain level of authority (i.e., disciplinarians); they were, in effect, "large and in charge." They didn't have to, and didn't want to, become friends with their students as they were supposed to prepare them for the world and their futures. However, in today's connected world, many students, especially those in middle schools and beyond, are living a public life and engage their teachers (and vice versa) before and after class using social media. Being "friends" on Facebook often leads to the ill-conceived student assumption that they are "friends" with their teachers at school. This means that the respect and authority that came with the title of "teacher" has now changed so that "friends" can help each other out and even be challenged or "dissed" in front of others. The expectations for social media connections have changed how in-person teacher–student relationships develop.

This redefined "friendship" also carries over into the retail world as many retailers are struggling with the ways in which they reference consumers. This struggle is noticeable when words like *client* (sounds too clinical for some) and *customers* (seems stale and overused) yield to newness in the word *guest*, referring to someone who is here temporarily in whom the host wants to promote return visits. Disney had this figured out long ago with their older media campaign, and now its restaurant experience depicted in advertisements also uses the catchy phrase, "Be Our Guest" effectively as it is repeated throughout the organization. Some retailers have also reverted back to the idea of "friends" as customers, but they also expect those "friends" to be "followers" of the product, service, or experience, even if they can't do so in person, right now. What we see is a shift from "right now" promotions to the online, never-ending, "always now" messages of a connected world. After all, what are "friends" for if not being readily available?

SOCIAL ANXIETY

In addition to the ways in which friends and friendships are defined, the prevalence of social media has also increased social anxiety among Millennials. While some members of each generation exhibit social anxiety, the Millennial generation often displays increased social anxiety and exhibits a heightened sense of uncertainty and avoidance when it comes to interacting in person with others, from friends to strangers. In fact, many employers notice how many Millennials have increased anxiety when making phone calls to potential employers or organizational contacts. This may ring true for many people across generations, but the rationale behind the anxiety varies. For example, Baby Boomers relied on telephones to access people from afar, as did the Silent Generation before them. Early Baby Boomers then passed this knowledge on to their Gen-X children even when newer technologies were introduced; they valued in-person conversations or person-to-person phone calls. However, many later Gen-Xers have fully embraced the technological advancements of the world and don't use their phones *as phones* as often as many older Gen-Xers do. In doing so, they reflect the culture's convenience strategy of electronic communications in the forms of texts, emails, and other messaging services, and these communication patterns are ones that most Millennials have picked up on and currently use most readily. Most Millennials may not even know their best friend's phone number because interaction is electronic or in person, and many don't know their own phone numbers because they are not expected to respond to a phone call or have others phone them. Many an awkward silence has occurred when two Millennials engaged in phone "conversation." The abilities of Millennials to hold meaningful conversations via phone have now been converted to Skype and other computer camera–ready exchanges. Skype allows a visual exchange or conversation to occur and nonverbal cues are used to interpret messages. Because many Millennials communicate via text messages, emojis (emoticons) have replaced the nuanced characteristics of punctuation and capitalization. When engaging others via phone, many Millennials aren't able to "read" the variations in others' voices and feel left out or lost. By using services such as Skype, Millennials regain some of their confidence as they can see the other person and use visual cues to establish meaning. In fact, Skype was a useful tool in the writing of this book as we were able to see each other virtually in person each week rather than solely conversing via phone. When phone calls were necessary, they were quite shorter and more task-oriented than our Skype conversations. We experienced this contradistinctive opportunity and are thankful to have embraced it despite our Gen-X tendencies toward interpersonal, face-to-face, in-person conversational exchange.

ACCEPTANCE VERSUS TOLERANCE

Despite their apparent social anxiety and uncertainty avoidance, Millennials also differ in the degree to which they tolerate and accept diversity. Much of this is the result of their late Baby Boomer and early Gen-Xer parents who supported civil rights and later LGBTQ rights. The advent of technology allowed those who identified themselves differently from cultural norms to organize and create online communities for support. Not only is technology a great support system, its use is an area for contradistinction across generations, with support groups varying across social categories (i.e., gender, sexual orientation, race). Prior to the 1970s, few freedoms were truly guaranteed by the United States and there were even fewer ways to reach others who were interested in change. Gays and lesbians and others were forced to be silent and closeted about their romantic (sexual) interests. If they were found out, they could be fired from their jobs or placed in psychiatric hospitals without much notice or support, or maimed or even killed. Those who wanted that lifestyle or were gender nonconforming had to live in secret and visit places that were available yet covert. For example, in the 1950s, the Blacklisting of Hollywood (McCarthyism[9]) included gays and lesbians as targets, while military edicts were put forth to force gays and lesbians into dishonorable discharges despite the recognitions they may have received during their service. The time of "free love" in the mid- to late 1960s opened some doors, but it wasn't until the pivotal moment of the Stonewall Riots on June 28, 1969,[10] that a gay and lesbian rights movement evolved. Early difficulties were resolved and despite continued resistance to marriage equality and gender nonconforming expressions, the Millennial generation has had access to a world filled with information and online communities to make the coming out process a bit easier; the levels of tolerance and acceptance have increased over the past few decades. Many more Millennials admit that they are aware of difference and accept that everyone has a right to be happy even if others deviate from current identified norms. In fact, we are witnessing more public representation of gender expression and identity than ever before with colleges seeking to make people who are "gender nonconforming" more comfortable. In Vermont, one college now has a third demographic option on its application for denoting gender,[11] and elsewhere some colleges have gender-neutral dorms[12] or bathrooms,[13] while others are still seeking ways to lessen the disparity non–gender-specific or trans people experience whether in an educational, workplace, or judicial setting. Imagine this type of acceptance or recognition during World War II or prior to 1969 or even today in some parts of the United States. As we wrote this chapter, the Governor of Indiana was under fire for a "religious freedom restoration act" that apparently provided outlets for LGBTQ discrimination,[14] and students at Duke University were protesting a noose left hanging from a tree on its campus.[15] Clearly, not all people or regions are as tolerant as others, and Millennials have been identified as the most open to diverse identities, despite the Dylann Storm Roofs (responsible for the Charleston massacre in June 2015) in the world. We noted earlier how this acceptance or higher tolerance affects their political and religious choices, and this should be noted as a priority for educators and employers alike.

A DELAY IN MARRIAGE AND FAMILIES

Another area where Millennials exhibit some contradistinctive beliefs and practices is in the covenant of marriage, not always in a strict biblical sense but in the sense of a contract or agreement between two people. Many believe in same-sex marriage and will protest others who don't recognize or support these marriages. With their more accepting and tolerant views on diversity and their own family experience, Millennials do have some different views about marriage and its timeliness. Many Millennials often come from divorced, single-parent homes, blended families, or witnessed their grandparents' divorce, and on average have delayed marriage and raising families. The 50 percent divorce rate that accompanies many news stories is also a myth. While it is true that Baby Boomers have the highest divorce rates, Gen-Xers' and Millennials' rates are declining.[16] Many Baby Boomers witnessed differences in opportunities granted and sought during the late 1970s and early 1980s; therefore, many marriages dissolved as many men and women sought to "find themselves." It was also a time of workplace opportunity as more women were entering the workplace and earning degrees, including a second-wave feminism movement that opened doors for many women from the workplace to education.[17] In fact, women were often the ones to leave those Baby Boomer marriages.

Gen-Xers also often experienced these marriage dissolutions and became wary of marriage themselves, often marrying a bit later than their Baby Boomer or late Silent Generation parents. Their divorce rate has decreased, partly because they marry later, and Millennials may also witness another decrease in the divorce rate over time. Several Millennials we interviewed were quite cautious when it came to marrying their partner. To be fair, they value marriage but want to be sure they are prepared for marriage both financially and relationally. Since most rely on their partners for serious advice on sensitive issues, most Millennials want to be sure they are financially solvent *prior to* getting married and believe that frank discussions of one's finances is paramount to successful marriages.

Because those late-marrying Gen-Xers remember their own childhood experiences with divorce and as latchkey kids, many have become overprotective of their own children and are more closely associated with the Snow-Plow Parents that we spoke of early in the book. Moreover, because early Gen-Xers and late Baby Boomers tend to be dual-career oriented, they also scheduled their children's lives around their own work lives. This led to Millennials being the most scheduled generation such that we witness their stress levels elevating from all of the expectations placed on them. Millennials often feel compelled to be doing something all of the time, and being connected 24/7 only exacerbates that feeling, thus leading to high stress levels and an increase in anxiety.[18] With all of these pressures and anxiety, marriage is often not a priority until financial and other types of stability are earned.

WORKPLACE

To be financially stable, Millennials are entering the workplace in significant numbers and their expectations for the ideal work environment are distinctly different. As previously mentioned, Millennials like a flexible workplace that allows them to be creative and productive when they are "with it" and aware (awake), not specifically between the hours of 9:00 a.m. and 5:00 p.m. They want, even demand, more feedback from their co-workers and superiors, are more willing to question authority, and expect promotions or other rewards for a job well done. This stands in direct opposition to the Silent Generation, Baby Boomers, and most Gen-Xers. Members of these generations often waited their turns, earned those rewards based on merit, and didn't typically expect to be singled out for accolades. While everyone enjoys accolades, not everyone demands them or seeks them out, except for many Millennials who are used to being told by their teachers (friends) and parents (friends) that they are doing a great job. Many Millennials identify the actual process for a task or project as most important when they say things like "I worked really hard on that" or "I tried to tackle that player." What we often see are Millennials who believe that trying is good enough. However, when asked to describe their process, many Millennials will finally admit that the way they approached the task or assignment wasn't the most effective way and the consequences for that are real. This doesn't mean that they will change their process, which often affirms the ongoing entitlement perceptions other generations have of them. This feeling of entitlement is certainly one way in which they are indeed contradistinctive.

RUNDOWN OF CONTRADISTINCTION

Millennials, although technologically embedded and often technologically advanced, see ways to connect with people and to challenge social and cultural norms and expectations, much like the generations before them. Being contradistinctive is an essential component of change, whether it is perceived or actual. There are demonstrated ways in which each generation wants to clearly distinguish itself from previous generations, despite the fact that there are similarities that occur in different life stages and contexts. Since Millennials are deeply committed to social media and personal advancements (as are many of their parents), difficulties in communication in and across generations can, at times, be problematic. Clear rules and policies are required to assist those technologically, deeply embedded people, to make room for and accept that not all interactions need to occur via text, email, or social media. There are times when deep interpersonal connections need to be made in person without technological distractions. On the other hand, those who aren't as technologically integrated or resist at all costs need to recognize that successful connectivity and relationships can, and do, develop online. They too need to make room for and accept that being connected via cell phones and tablets can lead to successful and productive exchanges between and among people. What is needed is a balance and recognition from all people that change *and* tradition are equally valuable in all aspects of life. Clearly, we don't always have to throw the proverbial baby out with the bath water to adjust to and engage an ever-changing world. But we do need to listen to each other to get started, so let's hear from Millennials firsthand.

Part III

Moving Forward: What's On the Horizon?

9

MILLENNIAL VOICES: "OUT OF THE MOUTHS OF BABES"

Fact or Fiction: Millennials have no clear sense of who they are or where they're headed.

MEET OUR MILLENNIALS

- DeAndre "Dre" Brown is a twenty-four-year-old university student interested in the lesbian, gay, bisexual, transgender, queer (LGBTQ) community, crisis communication, and also serves as the Public Relations Coordinator for Motor City Pride. A budding entrepreneur, Dre recently launched the Media Wise Public Relations and Marketing firm.
- Esa Cano, twenty-one, grew up in a small town in upstate New York. Currently, she is a college student majoring in communications with a concentration in public relations and advertising, and is also minoring in graphic design. She enjoys learning new things, eating delicious foods, making art, and spending time with her family.
- Kyle Derkowski is a twenty-seven-year-old software engineer living in the Washington, D.C., area with his wife. Dedicated to giving back, Kyle volunteers with his local church youth group and is an officer for the Virginia Chapter of Cure SMA (spinal muscular atrophy). He enjoys watching movies, reading about technology, and following his hometown team, the New York Giants.

- Valerie "Val" Granuzzo, twenty-eight, is a proud Millennial living the dream. Val loves Broadway musicals, happy hour, TV crime dramas, and her library card. She currently works as a marketing manager for a talent management software company.
- Blake Hayes, twenty-three, is currently working in search engine optimization and paid search. Blake enjoys spending time with friends and family, hiking and exploring nature, and learning new things. Leaning on his faith-based sense of optimism, Blake's ultimate goal is to leave the world in a better place than he found it.
- Ayad "Eddie" Kadhim is a twenty-four-year-old television news anchor, producer, videographer, reporter, and editor living in Missouri. Eddie is a driven and understanding Millennial who enjoys both the process as well as the journey to pursue his interests. Additionally, he also enjoys hearing about everyone else's journey along the way.
- Dana Lenseth, twenty-five, is a native of upstate New York. She earned a bachelor's degree in public communications and is currently a senior producer at a television station where she is responsible for daily editorial decisions and the overall quality of the on-air product.
- Andrea Mellendorf is a nineteen-year-old college student double majoring in public relations and communications. After graduation, Andrea hopes to use her degree to serve a nonprofit organization focusing on children and families. She is also interested in pursuing a graduate-level degree. An accomplished violinist, Andrea not only enjoys theater, Catholicism, tennis, and being an active member of her university's Public Relations Student Society of America, but also loves spending time in her hometown with her parents and three siblings.
- Leah Rodriguez is a twenty-four-year-old senior at a university in the Midwest where she manages the social media for her university's College of Arts and Sciences and is also the president of a national student organization. A self-proclaimed "professional recipe follower," Leah loves to bake and cook using her grandmother's recipes and others that she finds on Pinterest. Originally from California, she now spends time with her adoring fiancé Curtis.
- Marissa Salzone, twenty-four, was born and raised in Long Island, New York, and attended college in upstate New York. She is an online marketing manager for a personal injury law firm. In her spare

time, Marissa loves being outside and walking her French bulldog, Chi-Chi.

- Ann Than, twenty-eight, is a rehabilitation nurse who enjoys spending her free time traveling, reading, and with her family. Her long-term goal is to continue pursuing a master's degree in nursing.
- Caitlyn Tuzzolino is a twenty-five-year-old marketing director and entrepreneur. In addition to her full-time marketing position, she also owns two small businesses, East Avenue Marketing, where she specializes in marketing and graphic design, as well as Caitlyn Michelle Makeup and Fashion where she offers professional fashion services, including wardrobe styling, closet organizing, and personal shopping.
- Jackson Wang is a twenty-two-year-old video journalist living in the Hudson Valley. Born in Hong Kong, Jackson is an ambitious individual who is chasing the American Dream. In his free time, Jackson enjoys playing sports, reading books, and spending time with family and friends.

WHO ARE THEY AND WHERE ARE THEY HEADED? MILLENNIALS SPEAK

Millennials often get the short end of the stick when it comes to praise and accolades. In our experience, we recognize that many Millennials exhibit many of the negative adjectives associated with this generation (e.g., *lazy, disinterested, self-centered*), but we also have found that a larger majority don't, and in fact provide a sense of hope for a strong future. It is apparent that Millennials know who they are and where they are headed, which parallels the thinking of individuals from each generation that we have encountered. Millennials, first and foremost, despise labels but know those same labels can be useful—at times. They are constantly hearing about how entitled they are and how quickly they expect to make millions. However, Millennials are also rather astute when understanding their own beliefs, fears, dreams, and the ways in which they must work with people across generations to be successful. They want to make a difference in the workplace but also know they have to fight the stereotypes associated with their generation. Additionally, we have also learned that while Millennials say that they are collaborative, they don't necessarily mean that they like to formally work in groups, at least not in the way that groups have been identified in the past. Instead, they collaborate by interacting with others in search of feedback (in person or online). To get a better sense of who these Millennials are and where they want to be, we asked a handful of individuals to share their thoughts with us in personal interviews. Each of the interviewees is either pursuing or has completed a higher education degree, and so this population doesn't necessarily capture a broader cross-section of Millennials' views, nor is it intended to do so. Each of these Millennials agreed to participate in an interview after completing an online survey. We believe that it is important for the reader to understand how Millennials respond to certain questions in order to provide you with insights into their thoughts and views. We believe conversations between generations are a great way to improve our cross-generational relationships.

During each interview, participants were asked a variety of questions that emerged from the online survey, personal experiences, and from other information available about Millennials. These questions related to their beliefs, preferences, attitudes, and behaviors, including questions about "their" generation and other generations. Each of the following questions is followed by a response and a brief summary of each question.

Question 1: What characteristics define your generational peer group?

We asked this question to allow Millennials to reflect on their own generational affiliations and how they, and others, perceive their peer group.

While no one really likes labels, especially those that are negative, this group of Millennials didn't need reflective time to discuss how their peer group is perceived. What is interesting is that some of the Millennials noted the negative perceptions with which they are often associated, while others were quick to discuss the positive attributes Millennials bring to the table.

Caitlyn notes that her generation believes that "everything should come easy" and that everything is at the tip of their fingers. When things don't come easy, they get frustrated. She suggests that parents sometimes set this message early (think about our Snow-Plow Parent), and that the Internet and Google share some of that responsibility as well.

Andrea, our youngest Millennial, says that her generational peers are ambitious, eager to learn, and are willing to speak out against injustice. She is certain that social justice is a defining characteristic of Millennials. She also makes it clear that there is a certain level of negativity that other generations hold toward Millennials and she is upset about that, just like you will also see with Leah, Val, and Dana.

Kyle, an older Millennial, believes that his peers are conservative, college educated, and career oriented. We note that his experiences run contrary to the beliefs that many hold about Millennials as being more liberal and democratic in their views.

Marissa, emphatically, and without a hint of hesitation, says Millennials are "fast-paced," "tech-savvy," "trendy," and "motivated." Her descriptions echo many of the points emphasized regarding Millennials throughout the book.

Valerie says she identifies with Millennials, but has a lot of crossover with her parents who are early Gen-Xers. She suggests that her views in many areas are more closely associated with Gen-Xers than Millennials. She believes that Millennials are an open-minded, tech-savvy, laid-back, go-with-the-flow generation. Like her Millennial counterpart, Andrea, she also knows that some of the negativity about Millennials is accurate since each generation has individuals who are lazy and lack drive. She is quick to point out that although she understands some of the negativity associated with Millennials, it is still annoying to hear.

Dre notes that Millennials believe they know all the answers and have great ideas. He also admits that they depend on others for networking, and believes that they are an entitled generation, especially when they have worked hard and don't get rewarded.

Jackson indicates that Millennials are ambitious, but may not always have the right focus because of the presence that social media has in their lives. This generation is also willing to try new things and to take risks to get ahead. This fits with the entrepreneurial spirit that we discuss in chapter 7 and with Eddie's following comment.

Eddie believes that Millennials are adventurous, and he also added that they are hard working, even if they have to live at home because they can't make enough money to pay bills, loans, and rent in the current economy. He suggests that pursuing their passions may eventually become secondary because they have to, at some point, make more money.

Esa noted that Millennials are proactive in their pursuits of social justice issues, such as same-sex marriage. In support of this, she highlights that when someone has more education they often have a deeper understanding and concern for these issues. She doesn't fault those who don't pursue social justice because she knows that people's experiences and priorities differ. It is interesting that our two youngest Millennials emphasize social justice.

On the younger end of the Millennial spectrum, Blake notes that Millennials are passionate about what they believe and look to challenge the establishment. He also suggests that many Millennials focus on individuality and self-exploration, and that they make and maintain connections in different ways than other generations. We note that this push for individuality may contribute to the Millennials' dislike of labels.

Leah noted that Millennials are hard working, determined, driven, and goal oriented. She indicated that sometimes people from other generations "don't take her seriously" and this troubles her, as it did Val, discussed later.

Ann, an older Millennial, believes that Millennials have knowledge and perseverance, and want to pursue their education and get good jobs. She was the only one to suggest that Millennials like to travel, which is quite evident from their social media posts during everything from one-day road trips to formal vacations.

Dana, as did some of her peers, mentioned that Millennials are hard working go-getters, but also recognizes that some Millennials are lazy and entitled. She doesn't necessarily like this association and the negativity that it lends.

In summary, Millennials generally characterize their own generation in positive ways, just as those generations that preceded them. Most highlight how Millennials are often perceived negatively, with some even admitting that these may be properly applied to some. What becomes clear is that Millennials are firm in their perceptions about themselves and others, and recognize the role of technology in their lives and future.

Question 2: Which generation, if any, do you identify with?

We ask this question to allow Millennials to freely identify, or not, with some generational groups without the pressure of always aligning as a Millennial based on their age.

Some of our Millennials immediately identified with this generation, while others were a bit more reluctant to solely identify with a single generation, especially if they found themselves toward the older end. For example, Kyle states that he is on "the cusp," while Ann sees herself fitting more "Gen-X descriptions" since for her, "social media is the distinguishing factor." Blake thinks that the Baby Boomers have a work ethic similar to that of Millennials, or what he calls "Echoboomers." Dre also aligned himself more closely with some of the Baby Boomer descriptions since "they had to find their own avenues and their own niche." Caitlyn doesn't readily identify with any specific generation, while Dana doesn't enjoy being labeled a Millennial because of the negativity. Val more closely identifies with Millennials but sees "cross-over" with her parents' generation as well. Marissa, Jackson, Eddie, Esa, and Leah all identified as Millennials, while Andrea identifies with her parents and is hesitant to identify with Millennials, just like Dana. However, Andrea also suggests that Millennials need to "sell themselves as credible" to older generations and seems torn. Overall, Millennials do identify with others in many ways, but negative perceptions and claims about Millennials make some wary about that label.

Question 3: What challenges do you face when interacting with other generations or your own?

We ask this question to have Millennials reflect on themselves, and others, while also seeking to understand the claims made by previous authors about perceived generational differences.

In discussing the challenges Caitlyn faces with her own generation, she believes that many assume they are the "top at work," and "what they really need is a time to process." She notes that, "they don't get that"—"they" being other Millennials—and often struggles with her own peers when they refuse to listen. With this view, she doesn't see nearly as many challenges with older generations. However, Andrea, a self-identified "old soul," believes that the negativity from other generations can easily be refuted, but Millennials have to be proactive and need to be more credible. She feels that she is often "viewed as a child" by previous generations and struggles to change that perception.

Kyle agrees but sees himself "on the cusp" between two generations and notes how what he calls "older generations" have problems with terminology and technology, and have a slower speed of learning. With his own age group, he sees his own level of social media use as one potential challenge since some of his friends are more involved in it than he is. Jackson also acknowledges that the jargon, or what he calls "tone" or "slang," is a communication challenge with other generations, but he also notes that Millennials struggle with face-to-face interaction in general, so he really does try to encourage this type of interaction with his peers. Val agrees with Jackson and Kyle when she notices that with other generations, all of whom are generally hard working and determined, technology is often a challenge. Millennials embrace technology and use email, Skype, and texting to connect with others, even in the workplace, while older generations often prefer the face-to-face interactions. Interestingly, Val also owns up to the perception that the Millennials' expectation of individual rewards or recognition for their work is problematic for her when she interacts with other Millennials. Dana also admits that communication with other generations is challenging because they "often lack a common ground" to start from. However, she doesn't experience these same challenges with her own generation.

Marissa also sees challenges within intergenerational interaction but views it as one of "clash management." One way this clash happens is that the Millennials are not afraid to say, "No, no this is not part of my job," whereas older employees may not speak up as readily about tasks outside the scope of their job description. She also believes that older managers sometimes placate those who say "no" and don't immediately address the potential clash. In a sense, this ties back to our claim that the "Snow-Plow" approach with Millennials sometimes occurs in the workplace as well. Sometimes managers or supervisors want to clear the way for their co-workers.

Dre is more forthright when he makes it clear that older generations often assume that Millennials "don't know much" without ever really getting to know them. He does, however, state that other Millennials "think we have great ideas" and is also frustrated by the perceptions of older generations, but understands where some of that negativity is derived. Eddie adds that a "generation gap" exists and that history and time make a difference for specific generations. He, like Andrea, suggests that Millennials must earn their respect because this will help them in the workplace. Eddie also believes that "Millennials assume they know too much" and that this negatively affects their ability to listen to others.

Esa, in a different way than Jackson, Kyle, and Val, sums up her challenges with other Millennials by focusing on semantics or "word choice" for all generations. She is more patient with older generations, over her own peers, because she admires them for "trying to keep up" and for their perspectives on such things as saving money.

Blake aligns with Esa's views about older generations, but notes that although he and Baby Boomers share a philosophical mindset, their approach is different. One challenge that he, and others, has with other generations relates to social media. But among Millennials, Blake often struggles with their short-sighted focus and their belief that, "if it feels good, do it" doesn't always consider the effect on others. This affirms Dre's comment about Millennials thinking they "have great ideas."

Ann, as does Dre, identifies with the negative perceptions that other generations hold about Millennials. She says, "they think that we are young and don't know anything" and that "they are stubborn" and "want Millennials to meet them at their level." The challenges with her own generation include the economy and education, especially the need for them to "be better at critical thinking." Leah affirms both Ann and Dre when she discusses her grandparents as an example of how others "don't take her seriously." As for her own generation, she says that the methods Millennials use in making friends and when forming groups is problematic for her.

Within any generation, negative perceptions are difficult to accept. Each generation generally encounters some difficulty working and interacting with individuals spanning different age groups. What is clear to us is that we all need to approach intergenerational interactions with a level of patience in order for many of these challenges to be overcome.

Question 4: Distinguish a "manager" from a "leader."

We ask for this distinction because previous authors suggest that Millennials require continuous feedback and don't often understand or appreciate leaders.

In organizing the Millennials' responses to this question, we notice much similarity in their perceptions. Regarding this question, both Caitlyn and Leah begin by noting that managers shouldn't micromanage and should lead instead. They clearly see a difference between the two positions. Where they differ a bit is that Leah sees managers as being more hands-off while leaders are part of the team. She says, "A good manager is more of a leader. They don't tell us what to do and then go back to their office. Managers tend to give a task and then go back to their office." They both believe that managers have to be good leaders, and for Caitlyn, a leader is "someone who believes in the company and gives incentives."

Andrea adds to this conversation by attributing an ethic of care to a leadership position, with Marissa, Dre, and Dana also confirming this. Dana says that leaders are "listeners, compassionate, just, and organized." Being aware of the feelings of others and expressing concern about their well-being is important since doing so can lead to genuine respect and even strong personal relationships. Blake is a bit more hesitant to form close personal connections because this can lead to a muddled perception of the managers' and leaders' roles. He says co-workers, like children, should "be seen, but not heard. Don't get into personal topics like religion. Remain neutral with interactions."

The views from some of our other Millennials varied on this topic—as you might expect. Andrea states that as co-workers, leaders "step up if you need them to, but they don't take advantage" and they "give you something to learn." Dana adds that a manager is the same as a leader, but is more detached in order to see the big picture or the whole group. Kyle takes it one step further when he suggests that leaders tend to lead by example and are generally good role models. He believes that there is a balance between patience and listening, and that a leader must also be decisive when the need arises. For him, a good manager is the same as good leader, but also integrates intelligence (emotional and cognitive) and organization. Regarding co-workers, Kyle believes that they should display an unselfish attitude (in that they shouldn't always get their way) by being followers (where appropriate) and contributing equally to the job, and, perhaps more importantly, doing their job.

Val, however, is more focused on managers' and leaders' tasks in her distinctions. She believes that a leader is forward thinking, and should offer more than negativity by providing feedback, building relationships, trusting, and supporting others. Managers are responsible for the work and they need to be clear on goals, so they can align the whole to collectively accomplish those goals.

Dre concurs with Andrea, Marissa, and Blake about managers not being hoverers or micromanagers, but also adds the word "coaching" to the description. He says that coaches are there if you need them and you should be able to trust them. Sometimes, that may mean being a follower, just as Kyle noted previously.

Jackson, like Val, is clear in his distinctions. He identifies managers as problem solvers who need to be willing to speak up as needed. He defines leaders as individuals who offer input, listen, take suggestions, criticize, and are willing to be criticized. As co-workers, sharing ideas, listening, understanding, collaborating, and working at any level with others is primary. While leaders and managers do have some similar characteristics, Eddie notes that co-workers tend to push you and have the same level of talent, but can also share what they've done in order to help others, learn from them, and gain mutual respect, so managers may not do that.

Viewing this topic through a slightly different lens, Esa and Ann believe that leaders should be motivators, but for Esa, most importantly, they must acknowledge, accept, and celebrate differences. Managers must do the job well using open communication, while Ann believes that leaders must be the communicators. Esa is clear that not all managers are good leaders, and that all co-workers should be "dependable, willing to work with you, support each other and offer help."

These responses indicate that Millennials want to feel appreciated and want constructive criticism as needed. They want to work closely with their co-workers and want to build trust for completing work goals, but also seek out motivators who aren't always "hands-off."

Question 5: Do you like to work *in* teams or *on* teams? Here is the distinction we use: *In* is working or contributing as part of a whole, collaboratively, to achieve a common goal with dependencies and interactions on and with others. *On* is being part of a larger group working toward a common goal, but each piece is a separate responsibility.

We ask this question because there appears to be a gap between what many authors and researchers say about Millennials' desires to work in groups and our own experiences in working with Millennials in the classroom. This also includes the stereotyped assumptions that many hold of Millennials as a generation focused on individual rewards.

For this question, nine of the twelve Millennials state a preference to work *on* a team rather than *in* teams, and this also emerged as a clear preference in our survey. Andrea notes that "you get your own responsibility and you control your outcomes," while Marissa adds, "We want to be recognized for individual work." "The bottom line, it's all about individual efforts being recognized," notes Dre. Kyle says he also likes to work *in* team environments if he trusts that members are competent, but if they aren't, then he would rather work *on* teams.

The remaining three Millennials like to work *in* teams. Eddie preferred working in a team because "everyone is working toward one goal together, as a unit" and "it is easier to ask people for input and they are willing to help." Regarding being *on* a team, Leah indicates that some Millennials are less likely to help others "because it is not part of their job," which echoes Marissa's statement in question 3.

There is a common understanding that there is a real difference between working *on* a team or *in* a team. Other authors note that Millennials like collaboration, and while that is true, how they collaborate or want to collaborate doesn't necessarily follow the same traditional definition that many co-workers hold.

Question 6: Describe your ideal work and learning environments.

We ask this question to situate their views of what an ideal (productive) learning and workplace environment might look like. We believe that changes to the workplace and classroom are inevitable.

Learning Environment

In general, each generation has adopted and follows a particular style of learning, and Millennials are no different. The Millennials interviewed here prefer to learn in an open, interactive environment, and they also like personal contact within these same environments. Most don't prefer online learning over traditional face-to-face learning, and they also want to be involved in shaping their own educational experiences. At times, this may mean using online news sites and resources via a web browser, or using social media to complete assignments.

From the outset, many of our Millennials quickly indicate a preference for learning and working in person rather than remotely. Caitlyn prefers the traditional face-to-face learning environment because she can "soak it in better." Kyle mentions that this interactions allows him to "experience what teachers are talking about and he likes to do that on smaller campuses where he can also make friends." This same philosophy regarding the size of the in-person environment also resonated with Marissa and Dana. They are interested in an environment that is small and where teachers can "better understand their strengths and weaknesses." Andrea simply doesn't enjoy online learning because "professor interaction is needed" and she needs a "professor who can help." On the other hand, a number of our Millennials embrace the ideas of an online, hybrid learning component within their educational environments. Val likes a balance of online and in-person learning and Dre also likes a blend but doesn't like "old-school-style lectures" and enjoys participation and collaborative learning. Blake and Jackson both express an interest in "visual learning" with Blake adding that he prefers a more active learning that emphasizes doing, rather than passive listening.

What is clear from each response is that regardless of the medium, personal interactions and connections with the teacher seems to rise to the top in their preferred learning environment. This makes sense when we recall their desire for constant feedback and being, as Eddie says, "noticed."

Work Environment

Opinions on an ideal work environment may differ a bit since many Millennials don't believe that the workplace is really a place to learn. However, they do understand quite well that their productivity is directly affected by their work environments. Just ask Zappos or Google for some examples of a "nontraditional" working environment catered for today's workers.

In keeping the theme of a hybrid in-person and virtual working environment, Val indicates that her preferred working situation includes both online and in-person interactions. Dre focuses on the physical space where he prefers few closed doors in the office and an open space that allows for collaboration. He even mentions that he likes to see food, chairs, and decorations to liven the place up a bit. Jackson concurs and also likes a work environment that is conducive to group collaboration, is relaxed, and one where ideas are shared and accepted. Andrea, in shaping her response to this question, highlights her preferred working environment as akin to a coffee shop. She prefers a creative, open work environment with no cubicles. She expects ideas to be shared and heard, and Esa's opinion parallels this as well. She desires a workplace wherein she has the freedom to express creativity, but also indicated that deadlines are important. She also sees the need for some collaboration and some independence, and notes that it takes a particular type of office space to accommodate this. Leah also identifies closely with the need for collaboration and support in the workplace.

Interestingly, many of the responses to this question did not necessarily focus on the physical working environment, but rather on the components that contribute to the workspace as a whole. Marissa focused on how she wants to be treated in the workplace. She holds a "leave me alone until I need help" perspective and also desires her employers and co-workers to recognize others' workloads when asking for something. Eddie enjoys working with happy people, those who can be human despite their stress. He also prefers a boss who gives some independence once you have established yourself. Ann prefers good leaders and managers who help each other and are patient. She also needs technology, equipment, and training to remain relevant in her field. Dana wants a job where co-workers pull their weight, and, for her, the job determines the work hours. She would, however, be open to changes in such schedules. Finally, Blake notes that there is definitely a need for the traditional rank and power structure within the workplace, which aligns with his Baby Boomer admiration, but he also knows that these can inhibit performance.

What we tend to see as a result of this question is a need for work environments to continue to evolve and offer independence and guidance, environmental flexibility, and stability. These Millennials don't necessarily want things to stay the same, or to even change in some respects. Their ideal work environments appear to be situation dependent.

Question 7: If you do receive individual rewards, recognition, or accolades, then what do you want them to be?

We ask this question to confirm that rewards are desired and that the type of reward doesn't vary too much from what other generations want.

As noted earlier in the book, Millennials often seek rewards or recognition for a job well done. This desire is similar to prior generations and doesn't set Millennials apart simply because, let's be fair, we all like to be appreciated for something wherein we had success. For example, Kyle says that he doesn't seek out recognition but he doesn't turn it down when it happens because "if you feel worthy, you work harder." Andrea, Eddie, Blake, and Leah also like individual accolades, and something as simple as an employer or co-worker saying "good job" is appreciated. However, Leah points out that if feedback is negative, she would like to better understand the reasons for the negativity. Marissa would like to see rewards come in other forms as well, from free breakfast, early leave on holidays, or even a day off for your birthday. Dre is similar to Marissa and notes that if he works hard and doesn't get rewarded, "he doesn't feel valued."

Clearly, we all like to be noticed and valued in some way, and when it comes to learning and working, things are no different. As educators, we notice that a simple "Good Job" on a paper or a "thank you for your class participation" can go a long way with Millennials. This type of feedback can motivate students to continue on a strong path and this seems to extend to the workplace as well.

Question 8: What role do social media play in your work, personal, and educational lives?

We ask this question because the most obvious characteristic of Millennials is their connectedness, especially via social media. This question also asks them to reflect on the role of social media in three key aspects of life.

Work

Regarding the use of social media in the workplace, Caitlyn notes that she uses these platforms only when it is required of her. Andrea and Blake both indicate that social media is an extension of an individual and can be considered "an extension of the real world." Eddie uses Facebook to connect with his boss on a social level, but other Millennials are required to use social media in their daily public relations–, law–, and news-oriented careers. Val and Ann affirm that the use of social media isn't critical for their jobs, while Kyle tends to be very careful with his use of social media at his job, and he has to be, so he instead uses internal communications that he describes as "Facebook-esque."

Since jobs vary for these Millennials, their use of social media in the workplace is often dictated by their job responsibilities. What we don't see is much contact with employers and co-workers mentioned as important after the workday is completed.

Life

Each of our Millennials reaffirmed the importance of social media when it comes to connecting with family and friends. This make perfect sense, especially for this generation wherein connectedness is an expectation and cell phones are often given to children before they enter middle school. Kyle was the only one of our Millennials to say that he doesn't often post to his social media platforms, but likes to see what others are up to. Dana says that Facebook is important for setting up social gatherings and Val quite poignantly asserts that social media "is critical, and you're foolish to think otherwise." In a rare disagreement, Blake affirms that he rates social media low on his scale of importance and even disconnects after 10:00 p.m. He was the only Millennial to directly acknowledge this, even though Esa wishes that social media didn't play such an important role as it currently does in her life.

Nearly all of our Millennials rely on social media for connecting with others, and perhaps Blake is onto something when he says that he disconnects at night. Ultimately, social media will continue to remain relevant, until something better or different comes along, and we have to take greater care to manage and monitor our use on a personal level.

Education

In noting the importance and prevalence of social media within education, it was interesting to see that each Millennial was so focused on the roles that social media hold in their personal and working lives; only Caitlyn and Val responded to the educational element. Caitlyn doesn't believe that using social media within a classroom is important for her education, whereas Val uses it to connect with her peers for conferences. We can't draw any conclusions here other than perhaps social media is not as relevant to formal learning for Millennials as some may believe. We know that this generation uses sites like BuzzFeed, Twitter, and YouTube to get its news and learn about current events, trending topics, and viral videos, but what we don't know from their responses is where these fit in the classroom.

Question 9: What are your views about privacy?

We ask this question because we live in a world where public and private are blurred when technology offers convenience, accessibility, and efficiency for all we do.

We usually can't go a day without a news story discussing some system that was hacked or some type of accessibility scandal. Yet, with all of the concerns about wiretapping, cell phone data access, and other on-the-go apps and technologies, we wanted to know how Millennials feel about their privacy.

The majority of the Millennials that we interviewed are aware of and concerned about privacy settings in apps and social media, and they use them to have some sense of control over their lives. However, many take no extra precautions to secure their information and those who do predominantly do so because of their jobs. So, despite their fears, most admit they have nothing to hide and aren't using advanced security measures to ensure their privacy.

Question 10: What are your views about money? Do you save for the future? Why or why not?

We ask this question because we often hear that Millennials live life for the "now" and therefore don't think ahead to retirement or big expenditures, like a home. We also know that Millennials are accruing the most educational debt ever recorded.

In the current economic climate, one's goals and realities are often at odds. The same holds true for these Millennials. Caitlyn owns two businesses and works a full-time job at the same time. She uses what she calls her "career money" to pay all of her bills, including her student loans, but her side companies allow her to save for her future. Andrea is currently a resident assistant so she doesn't yet have an income but she plans on saving when she gets her first job. Kyle and Marissa save for their futures and their employers assist with retirement using standard work-sponsored retirement plans. Both value money but also deeply value other things, like family, too. Val describes herself as "very frugal" and says she gets this from her parents. She has paid off student loans and her car, and she tracks her finances using multiple financial platforms. She also wants her partner to be understanding of financial matters (on same page) so they can buy a house.

In reflecting on this question, Dre is honest and says that he saves for retirement because, "Social Security is not going to be counted on and government structure is limiting and not reliable." He holds off on large purchases and extra money goes into savings. Jackson's opinion differs in that he saves for everyday expenses and uses company savings for future, including buying a house. Eddie notes that he would love to save more but his student loans and everyday living expenses push the limits of his salary; and he won't settle down until he is financially secure, just like Val. Dana too is paying off student loans and a car, so she saves for those expenses while living at home.

Esa considers herself a big saver and she says this comes from her "working poor background." She gets anxious when she only has small amounts of money in reserve and acknowledges that she isn't like her peer group, Millennials, in this area. She even, at one point, charged her siblings interest on money she loaned them to assist them in learning about the value of a dollar. Blake too is a big planner because he knows how he wants to live; he has long-term plans and saves accordingly. He also acknowledges that basic needs come from first when considering one's finances. This same philosophy resonates with Leah as well because she wants to save, but any "extra money" goes to pay off school. Her partner assists her in planning for her future including her monthly expenses, and she is learning from this planning process. Ann too learned from a planning process, but her knowledge came from a *New York Times* article. She believes that Millennials need more financial awareness to avoid future pitfalls.

It should be easy to see from these responses that these Millennials really do think and care about their futures. They want to save for retirement and big purchases, but the current economic realities put those on hold and delayed gratification holds down impulse spending for a while.

Question 11: How important is education to you? Why?

We know that Millennials are the most educated generation to date; however, we ask this question to hear from Millennials about how they view education.

For Millennials in general, education is highly valued. Most of our participants reasoned that in order to have a good career, you must have a degree; some even suggested that you must always stay current in your field of interest. Caitlyn seizes "all opportunities" for education, Kyle suggests that multiple degrees "open doors," and Marissa says, education "helps with better jobs." Val takes this one step further when she reminds us that keeping current using outlets such as the popular TED talks and the *New York Times* add greatly to her ongoing informal education.

There are also those who take the approach of bettering oneself based on the experiences of prior generations. Dre, Esa, and Leah, who all come from working-class backgrounds, state that they desire to overcome what their elders have had to struggle with to achieve success. Dre notes that his degree may not be enough, while Leah says that education is her "golden ticket." For Esa, "learning is a passion," not an end goal. Resonating this same thought, Blake remarks that education doesn't always have to be formal because it can come from experiences, perhaps travel, a book, or other outlets.

Regardless of their backgrounds, these Millennials value education and find it extremely important. Perhaps this is why so many Millennials assume that they must go to college to be successful. This may also offer some insights as to why they are willing to undertake so much debt to do so.

Question 12: What are your views about religion?

We ask this question because there are reports about the growing number of Millennials who are "nones" (have no religious affiliation) in the United States.

The responses related to this question may come as little surprise to many. Andrea, Kyle, Blake, and Leah hold their religions close, while the other Millennials wouldn't consider themselves deeply involved with religion at this point in time. Caitlyn believes that "you should have a belief of some sort," while others may not currently practice the religion that they grew up with because many of their beliefs are at odds with the particular beliefs favored by their respective religions. Dana was encouraged by her parents to embrace religion while growing up, but finds it difficult to keep up as she continues on her life journey. One participant believes that the Bible is "man-made not God-made" while others believe in a higher power but also believe that religion is a personal choice and should be individually determined, even if their parents raised them within a particular faith. In fact, Blake believes many people say they are "faithful" but "not religious" because they are apprehensive about how others may view them. Ann concurs with this view and notes that "religion is a sore topic for many."

We can see that, in general, Millennials regard religion as being important but that one's views must not be pushed onto others. Religion is personal and doesn't have to be made public.

Question 13: What are you views about marriage?

We ask this question to delve further into marriage trends that indicate that fewer people are getting married or stay married.

What we discovered from our Millennials is that marriage is very important to them, but both the timing and definition of marriage has evolved from those practiced in previous generations. The vast majority of the Millennials that we interviewed are waiting to marry until they find the right person, have achieved financial stability, or both. The fact that some of these Millennials say "if" the right person comes along means that many aren't currently actively seeking "Mr. or Mrs. Right."

Question 14: What are your views on social issues and diversity?

We ask this question to garner insight into how Millennials view these areas. If they are self-centered, then we thought there might be a contradiction present in social justice advocacy. Additionally, Millennials have been called the most diverse and accepting generation. Sometimes the interviews went in a new direction and we were unable to ask this question. When we did ask it, nine Millennials responded.

The idea of social justice is one that has been heavily discussed in our media over the past years. From Ferguson, Missouri, to Charleston, South Carolina, race (and racial equality) has been one of the most important social issues of our time. Let's simply take into account the Supreme Court's 2015 discussion regarding gay marriage or the public discussion of Caitlyn Jenner and we can quickly recognize that there are countless social issues to discuss. Millennials are often the first generation to speak out against injustice. Sometimes they do that via organized rallies, while other times they may defer to social media (Blake and Ann mentioned this in their responses). The main topic of discussion regarding social justice during our interviews related to marriage. Andrea, Val, Dre, Jackson, and Leah all place this topic as a primary interest. Each supports the right to marry, even if, as Val says, it may be "at odds with a religious upbringing." Each individual also encourages a heightened level of open mindedness related to the topic, including Eddie who says, "Just care about and accept people more." Jackson agrees with his Millennial counterparts and adds that economic inequality, as identified by social justice groups like the Occupy Movement, is another important issue that can be attributed to this topic.

On the contrary, Esa approaches this topic from a vastly different perspective as she speaks directly to social justice and uses it to characterize her own peer group; she does, however, stop short of attributing her views to Millennials in general. She generally finds challenges in social justice and awareness when discussing word choice or policies with others who may not be directly in her own group of friends. Dana goes one step further when she asserts that we are "naïve to think that equality exists."

From these responses, it is clear that many Millennials are more open-minded regarding the topic than previous generations. However, we can't be naïve to think that we live in a postracial or post-LGBTQ society. Too many world events occur on a daily basis to give us a dose of reality and remind us that not everyone is created equal or even has equal opportunities.

Question 15: What will your generation be most remembered for?

We ask this question because, if Millennials are focused on the here and now, then questions related to the future may be difficult to answer.

The responses to this question are variable and all over the map. We have learned that there are certain themes that characterize this generation, and these are also reflected within the following answers. In the words of Millennials, this generation can be described by the following phrases or adjectives:

Technology-Based Responses

- The Internet generation
- Technology experiential growth
- Information access and creativity
- Lifestyle improvement
- Making things go viral
- Social media
- Social media activism

Change Agent–Based Responses

- Open-minded
- Contributor in the workplace when older people retire
- Move toward equality (people as people)
- Fight for gay rights
- Revolution, protests, change, awareness of societal negativity
- No satisfaction or happiness even with everything at our fingertips
- "Hang out" rather than "play"

Other Recurring Messages

"We are NOT all lazy."

Ultimately, what we recognize as a result of these responses is that Millennials see themselves as tech-savvy and tend to identify with technology in one form or another as a distinguishing feature of their generation. They embrace this feature rather than run from it.

Question 16: From whom do you seek advice? And on what issues?

We ask this question in honor of our Snow-Plow Parents who want to clear the way for their children. Note that advice should not be confused with the actual "doing"!

Millennials often seek advice from either a close family member, their current partner, or both; however, the topics that they seek advice on generally define the target audience. Caitlyn and Andrea are very open individuals with no topics off limits in discussions with their family members. Kyle, on the other hand, tends to look more to his partner for general advice, but if the advice is medically related, he seeks out his mother. When he is interested in gathering an opinion related to life decisions, Kyle seeks out his father's advice instead. Marissa sees her family as an anchor and heeds their advice for everything from work, financing a car, schooling, and personal issues, but also notes that if she was married she would discuss these with her partner. Like Marissa, both Val and Dana also have close relationships with their families, and Val seeks her family's input for everyday issues. However, when it comes to career-related advice, she saves these discussions for her friends. Jackson seeks job-related advice from friends and family, but relationship issues are strictly reserved for his friends. In contrast to most, Dre doesn't engage his family with many topics, but rather relies on his partner for advice. Eddie has a different plan as he engages his own issues through self-reflection, only turning to his father if he needs to consider a nonemotional topic. Ann recognizes that she would discuss any topic with her partner were she to marry, but reserves confidential items for her friends. The one exception to this rule is that she will discuss big life decisions with her family, just like Kyle noted previously.

In the end, Millennials seek advice from a variety of sources and advice seeking is situational and relationally dependent. It is not surprising that most of our Millennials seek out their families for support given that so much of what they have learned comes from interactions and shared experiences that resulted from time spent with them.

Question 17: What matters most to you?

We ask this because one embedded assumption noted by authors previously writing about Millennials is that the generation just doesn't care about others; in other words, many assume narcissism reigns supreme when discussing Millennials.

A quick summary of the responses provided to this question highlight that family and friends are of the utmost importance to Millennials. Couple this with their desire for happiness at home, work, and play, and we soon realize that Millennials may be able to help all of us relax a bit. Other phrases that we captured related to what matters most to Millennials include "work–life balance," "job satisfaction," "treating people as people," and "education."

Question 18: Any additional comments?

We ask this question to allow Millennials an opportunity to express themselves further or elaborate on a previous question. Only a small handful of our Millennials took this opportunity.

In the words of the Millennials, "We mean well and we want to make things right; we want to make a difference." Members of this generation also recognize that "we are different, trend-setting and the base for new work setting." "We care about, and accept people more, and also recognize that Millennials will make a tremendous case study." Each of these additional comments remind us that every Millennial has unique ideas and insights.

So what does this all mean? Well, these voices tell us that Millennials aren't all the same, just as all Baby Boomers or Gen-Xers aren't the same. We see that while some of their comments fuel the fire for attributing some of the aforementioned stereotypes and assumptions about their generation, Millennials are a unique bunch. The few Millennials who find themselves at the older end of this generational range tend to identify more with their Gen-X counterparts, while the youngest of the Millennials actively embrace social change. Those in the middle, in general, exhibited similar views related to the three major areas (life, work, and education) that were the focus of our discussion. Ultimately, Millennials, like the generations that preceded them, will have various distinctive accomplishments to rest their hats on, but many of these will also resemble, in some ways, their age counterparts' successes from previous generations. We are all different, but more similar than we would like to initially believe.

10

EMBRACING THE CHALLENGES AHEAD

Fact or Fiction: Disengaging is our only option.

GETTING THE MOST OUT OF MILLENNIALS

We have established that Millennials do indeed elicit certain characteristics, as do all prior generations in their own way. Millennials are connected, confident, and cavalier—in an "old-school" sort of way. They are an outspoken, self-assured, entrepreneurial, "pain in the ass," somewhat contradistinctive bunch with numerous talents. They are also quite comfortable challenging the traditional ways of doing something (change agents) in the classroom as well as in the workplace, and are the most tech-savvy group to date. However, we have also learned that when it comes to many of the core beliefs practiced by prior generations, Millennials are not as different as we think, especially at their current ages. So what does this mean as we move forward? Now that we know who the Millennials are and how they operate, what are some ways that generations can better work together and adapt, as needed, to be more effective? What will help "keep the peace" at home, in the classroom, and in the workplace, yet not destroy the basis on which these institutions were built? The following are some specific thoughts to consider for parents, teachers, employers, and co-workers.

PARENTS

1. Aid in the modeling of beliefs, behaviors, and attitudes for your children, but then allow them to complete tasks on their own, even if it ultimately ends in failure. Without learning that failure is healthy, Millennials will set themselves up for a future of frustration when they finally experience failure, yet aren't equipped to handle it.
2. Don't over-protect them—put the snow plow away and identify ways to enable your children to problem-solve and reap the consequences of their behaviors, good or bad. Learning these coping skills will allow them to better understand and anticipate consequences, in turn helping them prepare more effectively for adulthood.
3. Encourage your children to succeed, but don't promise them the world! Keep in mind that most Millennials will not achieve all goals that they set for themselves. This is an impossible expectation. If you can afford opportunities for them to take risks, then do so, but telling children that they can achieve anything at any time may not be appropriate.
4. Be realistic, not idealistic. Help them understand and identify their strengths and weaknesses, and then help them set achievable goals. Do your part to encourage some risk-taking in order to stretch their abilities and develop key strengths, but remember that each child has different abilities.
5. Emphasize the process and the outcome. Remind them that working hard doesn't always result in positive outcomes. For example, spending five hours on a school project doesn't always mean the project will earn an A. Be clear that not everyone should get a trophy or reward for working hard.
6. Take an interest in your children but don't always take over their lives. This means that you can be close with your children, but avoid building friendships that put you on equal footing in all situations, especially when they are young. This often transfers to other settings, such as the classroom or workplace.
7. Teach them to honor diversity in all facets of life so they will learn to experience diversity without blinders on. We live in a diverse world and to develop biases against others due to differences is

not healthy. Prepare them to "agree to disagree" at times when beliefs and values run counter to social expectations and to use their political voices and actions to make real change.

8. Teach them to engage with people both in person and virtually because flexibility and balance are keys to success. Help them learn to have conversations with people of all ages and teach them how to listen to others. Listening is a skill, not an innate ability.

9. Teach them to respect themselves and others. Learning about other generations and cultures leads to a better understanding of themselves.

10. Build character and personality, not one or the other. It is important to be thoughtful and to develop a personality. Building virtual personas shouldn't stray far from their actual personas. Children need to think before they speak (or post) and learn about how being liked by others doesn't always mean it is in their best interest.

11. Provide exposure to educational and cultural opportunities, but don't overschedule children's lives. Teach them that being "bored" is completely okay, and to learn to do things without the aid of technology.

12. Identify stress-related factors in their lives and teach them how to manage their stress. Stress will only increase as they get older and if they don't learn how to manage it early on, they are at increased risk for major health issues.

EDUCATORS

1. Avoid being friends with your students and certainly don't "friend" them on social media until they are no longer your students, unless you have an established mentoring role in their lives. Students of all ages may have difficulty understanding the different roles that you have inside and outside of the classroom, and their expectations of friends probably differs from their expectations of teachers.

2. Monitor social media even if you aren't "friends" and get parents involved with their children's social media use too. From Face-

book and Twitter to Yik Yak and Instagram, this exercise is important for both your own and your students' well-being. Handle inappropriate posts with care. We are all aware that social media can become an avenue for bullying and verbal rants.

3. Be flexible and adaptable to changing classroom environments by knowing your discipline and material, and seeking innovative content-delivery systems. You don't have to bow to students' needs and wants, but there are always opportunities for educators to become better at what they do, especially in an outcomes-based educational environment.

4. Don't erase all classroom traditions. Instead, explain why those traditions are important and how they can help prepare students for their futures. For example, lecturing is important for the development of good listening skills. Listening continues to be fundamental to success in today's world, technological or not.

5. Provide feedback to students for their successes and failures because constructive criticism goes a long way toward their learning. Don't always thank or congratulate a student for a job well done without providing ways for them to improve. Identify weaknesses in students who don't do well and also provide them a roadmap for improvement.

6. Identify a few ways to meet students "where they are" so as to keep them engaged in their own learning, but don't "throw the baby out with the bathwater" in doing so. For example, use your creativity to "reward" them for their efforts by allowing them access to a class Twitter feed or website that you have designed. Or use Instagram or Vine videos to end the class and post on a closed Facebook group just for them. It might even enhance a lesson.

7. Don't always be the sole "performer" or "sage on the stage" in the classroom. There are times when inviting students to lead, critique, and problem-solve is best-suited for them to become self-sufficient and interested learners.

8. Provide opportunities for students to engage materials at various levels, including rudimentary memory learning and problem-based learning. As educators, we know that students learn differently. Therefore, it would benefit us to offer multiple learning opportunities rather than emphasize or use only one type.

9. Be proactive in ways to evolve from "sage on the stage" to a more engaged interaction. Remember that you don't need to perform in a theatrical or comedic sense to engage them. Form sharing networks with your colleagues to see what they are doing in the classroom. Use online resources to gather ideas from people near and far.

10. Distinguish students' processes from their products so that they learn that working hard does not necessarily translate into an A if the outcome is insufficient. The earlier they understand this, the better off they will be when dealing with issues outside the classroom.

11. Address the role of social media in their lives and assist them in identifying ways to manage their connectedness and recognize its influence on the learning process. If we don't at least acknowledge the prevalence and convenience of social media and other technology in their (and our) lives, then we fail as educators to stay current.

12. Consider ways to be a role model in the classroom; practice what you preach. If you expect them to listen, then be a good listener as well. If you want them to learn new things, then you must learn new things too.

EMPLOYERS

1. Give, expect, and receive feedback, because being in touch with Millennials goes a long way toward keeping them motivated. Millennials want and even demand feedback throughout their workweeks. Feedback doesn't involve hovering or offering only negative commentary. Constructive criticism goes a long way.

2. Establish social media policies for the organization and invite them to participate in the creation or revision of the policy as appropriate. It is one thing to impose policies, but it's another to build those policies together. When technology changes, policies may need to evolve as well.

3. Provide a more level playing field, where possible, for everyone to be a leader in the workplace. Review chapter 3 to get a better sense of how to do this with an emphasis on coaching and alterna-

tive-service leadership. Keep up with the changing dynamics of workplaces. Consider speaking with other employers about their workplace successes. This can translate into a sense of motivation for employees and may even lead to more productivity.

4. Acknowledge a job well done. Doing so builds confidence, motivation, and loyalty. It doesn't have to be large bonus (that doesn't hurt); it can be a personal email message or even a thank-you card. If there is an opportunity to thank a team, then consider breakfast, lunch, or dinner as an option. Remember, you do not have to wait for the completion of the job; instead provide feedback along the way and help guide them as necessary.

5. Distinguish being *on* a team from being *in* a team to allow all generations to take part in workplace settings and feel valued as part of the organization. Explain to all employees the value of both types of collaboration. Some may be hesitant to shift their thinking about collaboration but being effective role models goes a long way in developing company morale.

6. Assign "coaches" for new employees where possible so that they can inquire about and begin to better understand the culture of the workplace. These coaches can be anonymous mentors via social media or in-person mentors who learn from and about others on a regular basis. The exchange of ideas and the development of relationships in the workplace is what is most beneficial here.

7. Offer flexible work hours where appropriate. Since Millennials are generally connected 24/7, they may work best from 12:00 to 4:00 p.m. and 7:00 to 11:00 p.m. in the same day. Some jobs may require a 9:00 a.m.–5:00 p.m. set-up, but many jobs maintain strict hours because it has been the tradition in the workplace. If productivity can be improved, then consider flexible work hours.

8. Try new office furniture or office arrangements to bolster creativity and avoid the "silo" mentality that occurs in some organizations. Look to other workplaces for ideas about how to stimulate productivity. Google and Zappos are great places to start.

9. Offer team-building opportunities using community work-projects, such as Habitat for Humanity, or promote external causes such as literacy or poverty initiatives. Developing a connection

with the community often targets employees' ethic of care in small yet meaningful ways.

10. Acknowledge the prominence of social media in the workplace and in employees' lives and then discuss ways to increase productivity without compromising company values. Having open discussions online or in person about these issues can go a long way to employees feeling "heard" and "valued" in the workplace.

CO-WORKERS

1. Avoid negative stereotyping of others no matter how old or young they are. We offered ways in which each generation comes with "baggage" based on their lived experiences. However, not all members of a generation or cultural group will fit assumed stereotypes.

2. Engage in team building with all co-workers, not just those in your age group. Have lunch or coffee with someone you don't know, and maybe even make it tech-free. Get to know others so they can get to know you. Organize an after-work event for *everyone*, not just those chosen few you always meet with on Fridays.

3. Embrace, rather than avoid, face-to-face *and* social media connections with Millennials and others. Try not to forego one in favor of the other. Seek opportunities to have a genuine conversation in the hallway or to send a quick text to a fellow employee to brighten his or her day. Sometimes just feeling recognized can make others reciprocate. This is *never* a bad thing!

4. Remember that age doesn't determine expertise and ability in all situations and that sometimes younger people know more about a topic or area than you might initially think. We often believe that with age comes experience. If we reshape this idea into one that means "any age," then we may begin to see what each person, despite his or her age, can offer.

5. Some Millennials may feel entitled, and may be lazy and overconfident at times, but they have been raised that way. They may need guidance and coaching, not deceit or disgust, from their co-workers. Think back to the challenges you faced when you were

their age or in their position. Was there anything others could have done differently to assist you? If so, then help them now.

6. Millennials can be entrepreneurial, highly creative, and confident, and are often excited about the work challenges they may face. Therefore, keeping a "finger on their pulse" can go a long way with their productivity and acclimation to the workplace. As with any relationship, find common ground.

7. Give feedback to everyone at various times, not only when something is done wrong or only at yearly appraisals. Too often, co-workers give feedback only at assigned times or when something needs improvement. Offer feedback (positive and negative) as things progress, and do so in respectable ways, not through insults and personal chiding.

8. Get to know Millennials before judging them; you may find them quite acceptable!

These tips and suggestions are only a starting point in relating to Millennials. We recognize that it is not everyone else's responsibility to ensure a Millennials' happiness and growth. Millennials have *a great deal* of work to do as well, and might consider the following when interacting with parents, educators, employers, co-workers.

MILLENNIALS

1. Note that age or time spent on the job does indeed have some importance in the workplace, classroom, and home. Don't disregard potentially useful information or relationships based on the premise that newer is always better. Sometimes that is just not accurate.

2. Engage and communicate with others both face-to-face as well as virtually. Both are necessary and the former can alleviate miscommunication that may occur in 140 characters or less, or via emojis.

3. Be confident in what you know and don't know, and remember that learning is an ongoing, lifelong, process. Condescension never works.

4. Learn to think on your own and problem solve. When you are stuck, don't look for someone to find the answer for you. Conduct some research and try to solve the issue before calling in your parent, teacher, or boss.

5. Know the difference between working independently and the right time to ask for help. Don't assume that others know what you need.

6. Prepare to work *on* teams and team-building projects. Working with others in most workplaces is inevitable, even if it means email exchanges or Skype sessions. Being *on* a team means that you should know what others are doing and they should know what you are doing. The end goal can't be accomplished without each piece being done well.

7. Prepare to work *in* groups with your co-workers toward achieving one common goal. If someone is struggling, engage that person and assist as needed. If the work is subpar, then encourage conversations with the whole group about ways to improve the process. As always, ask a manager or leader to speak to that person in a one-on-one setting if the subpar work continues.

8. Recognize that not all classrooms or workplaces can adapt to your preferred times for working efficiently. Some jobs actually do require you to be present between the hours of 9:00 a.m. through 5:00 p.m. or 8:00 a.m. through 4:00 p.m. Where possible, begin discussions about flexible working hours by focusing on productivity, not on mere desire to work later.

9. Be patient. Not everyone processes information in the same ways. Just as you learn differently from others, they also learn differently from you. Remember the old adage "old dogs can't learn new tricks" is not always true as many "old dogs can learn new tricks." It may just take a bit longer than you had planned.

10. Admit that technology doesn't solve *all* problems. You must look for alternative ways to solve them. Recognize that learning isn't simply about "looking things up"; rather, it is also about applying knowledge, using problem-solving skills, and being critical thinkers. If your GPS fails, can you read a hard copy of a map to get you to the destination?

11. *Fast* answers and solutions may not always be the *best* answers or solutions. So often Millennials think if they can find something

first, that information should be used. However, solutions aren't always best found quickly. They should be vetted with other possibilities.

12. Know the difference between opinions and facts, and between needs and wants. So often we think what we want is what we need. For example, I may think I *need* the new iPhone but the current one really does its job; therefore, I really only *want* the new iPhone. The same goes for opinions and facts. I can have an opinion about something but the facts may not support that position.

13. Don't rely on autocorrect or autodictation to do your writing for you and be sure you can write clearly, concisely, and accurately. Too often, we allow Siri or some other tool to speak on our behalf. Many times it is incorrect. Do you remember how that last email that autocorrected made you blush?

While we are sure there are many other tips we could provide, each relationship, person, and context varies, so these are just a few to get you started on a healthier interactive road to engaging others across generations. Our last suggestion is to now look ahead and ask "What do we need to be aware of when considering the next generation, the Neo-Millennials?"

WHAT'S NEXT? "FORGET ABOUT" MILLENNIALS; THINK NEO-MILLENNIALS

Fact or Fiction: Neo-Millennials are the same as Millennials.

What about those darn Neo-Millennials? Will these expectations become the new standard?

With the current population focused on nurturing their evolving relationship with the Millennial generation, society often forgets that there is another generation that is following closely behind and making waves of their own. While the approximate years have not yet been confirmed for this next generation, we can still ask, "Will this generation be worse or better than its Millennial counterparts?" Only time will tell, but let's quickly assess this new generation.

WHO ARE THEY?

Born to mostly late Gen-Xer and early Millennial parents, the next generation is commonly referred to as *Neo-Millennials, Post-Millennials,* or *Generation-Zers.* This generation will be even more connected and technologically savvy than their predecessors. Born in the early 2000s, these NEOs will most likely develop some norms and behaviors that individuals from other generations may have not experienced. Let's take a couple of moments to reflect on some of the behaviors that could be expected from the NEOs.

First, it is an expectation that they will spend less time watching TV in real time (live), if at all. They will most likely use on-demand features or streaming services to catch their favorite shows.

Second, NEOs will be much less likely to read books in the traditional printed form. Don't get us wrong. Books will not be disappearing; however, this generation has already incorporated reading technologies like Leap Frog, Nabi Big Tab, or other tablet or computer apps to help them learn to read on their own. As they grow older, there is also a preference to use these same technologies to read the digital versions of a book rather than a physical bound copy.

Third, they will use streaming opportunities to view movies. While some may still go to a movie theater for special viewings like IMAX or 3D, most will watch movies on-the-go or at home via devices such as Roku or Apple TV. They will also use the capabilities of their smart TVs to directly access services including Netflix, Amazon Video, Hulu, and other streaming services.

Fourth, many will have access to tablets, laptops, cell phones, and other tech gadgets at a much earlier age than previous generations. Many toddlers are using their parents' devices to keep them occupied in the supermarket, at home, or elsewhere. Parents are even providing these technologies to the NEOs at an earlier age than the Millennials. After all, many cars now come equipped with Wi-Fi to keep people connected, even while on the road.

Fifth, NEOs will be asked to be technologically savvy in the classroom at a much younger age than the Millennials, and be required to use laptops or tablets to complete their homework and engage in classroom activities. This could certainly lead to a much larger digital divide between school districts as we move forward. Some schools will have funds to offer these services, while others simply will not.

Sixth, many NEOs may become much less comfortable with in-person communication due to their reliance on technology as a preferred avenue for conversation. They will be more accustomed to texting than any other generation before them, and many will have spent more time using FaceTime or Skype with key people in their lives.

Seventh, NEOs may decide to avoid costly debt associated with college degrees as they witness their own parents' financial struggles. This will potentially lead to an evolution in how colleges are run and what they offer, and how much they will charge for their services. We may even see a decrease in the interest for "liberal arts" in favor of more technical and vocational majors.

Eighth, NEOs will continue to evolve the way in which organized outreach and protests occur in real time due to the effectiveness of social media activism. While more "live" protests have occurred in the last year across the United States, many more NEOs are turning to social media to support causes via hashtags, Facebook likes, and profile pictures (e.g., demonstrating support for LGBTQ rights via pride flags masking Facebook profile pictures after the Supreme Court ruled in favor of same-sex marriage in June 2015).

Ninth, NEOs may make even more demands of their employers' accessibility, teachers' responsibilities, and parents' friendships than ever before. Millennials are currently establishing a baseline and NEOs are not likely to stop the push.

Tenth, this generation will require a continued evolution of parenting, educational, and management styles, just as prior generations have done. As with any generation, change will continue to occur and affect all institutions, from the family to the classroom and into the workplace.

What is clear is that each generation is influenced by previous generations and by how they and their parents or guardians were raised. It is safe to say that technologically, changes will happen. Perhaps *The Jetsons* will become a reality, as robotic development continues. Children raised beginning in the 1990s and later have experienced the ability to watch DVDs in the car or use the car's Bluetooth or Wi-Fi systems to connect their LeapFrog devices, tablets, or other entertainment options. At home, many NEOs may not necessarily have a TV in their room, but they will have their portable devices with streaming capabilities to access their desired programming at any time. The days of children staying up using a flashlight to read a book at night are numbered as they can now use an app on their phone or tablet to accomplish this for them. They may even prefer to listen to a podcast where the books are read to them instead of reading them by themselves.

As a result of this exercise, it is clear that many more questions emerge than solutions offered when thinking about the future and the upcoming generation. The following section is our attempt to capture who we think this next generation is, will be, and could be, and how we might prepare for them in our homes, classrooms, and workplaces.

THE SEVEN—RATHER, EIGHT—CHARACTERISTICS OF NEOS

Fact or Fiction: NEOs will be even more connected than Millennials.

As previously highlighted, Millennials are always "connected." We believe that the level of connectedness that NEOs require will change, despite the advent and inclusion of new mobile technology and services. Maybe a better question that we should be asking here is, "Are NEOs unconnected?" Children are and will continue to learn and use electronic devices before they can walk; this is pretty much a given. They will continue to learn the importance of being connected and will demand (expect) that they be connected at all times. More children will sleep near their devices than ever before, and parents may adapt to this shift by sending text messages to wake them for school. They may have more difficulty with sleep as fear of missing out increases and they may even struggle with paying attention for any extended length of time. This can make the exercise of listening a challenge in all contexts.

While Millennials are already exhibiting this attention-oriented challenge, NEOs may well exhibit a heightened level of attention-deficit difficulties, while the request to find information very quickly using technology could make problem-solving more difficult for some NEOs, especially when an Internet search doesn't yield the desired information. However, there are some indications that their level of technological connectedness may lessen as they age once they begin to notice how their interpersonal skills are diminishing. This may lead to increased interpersonal contact outside of technological avenues, ultimately leading to a more balanced technology communication–interpersonal communication outcome.

Another way that NEOs will be different is that while many educators currently struggle with incorporating the use of the Internet, apps, social media, and mobile technologies into the classroom, their students already have a higher degree of expectations than their Millennial counterparts. Many schools, where appropriate, provide their students (starting in middle school or earlier in some cases), laptops or tablets with relevant apps, activities, and select electronic books or readings. Some even use Quick Response scan codes for "Open Houses" so that parents and other visitors can use their smartphones to access a video presentation of their child's work. An expectation will begin to be set for students to become computer literate and work with these integrated features on a daily basis.

As educators, we hope that teachers continue to develop problem-solving skills with their students, not merely information literacy. However, to accomplish this, teachers will need to embrace an evolution of teaching philosophies throughout classrooms across the country to make this successful. Millennials with Snow-Plow Parents expect easy solutions and become quickly frustrated when the answers aren't readily available or aren't easy to access. NEOs will need to learn valuable skills from their teachers and parents to properly equip themselves with the tools to be successful in the home, in the classroom, and in the workplace. Educationally speaking, the U.S. implementation of a Common Core curriculum to school districts across the nation will continue. Increased accountability may indeed mean resorting to "old-school" style of instruction wherein a particular test gauges knowledge and not necessarily "know how." This debate and the role of educators will have to be closely followed and assessed.

Fact or Fiction: NEOs will be contradistinctive.

As time progresses, it is quite possible that NEOs may indeed look very similar to Millennials as many of their characteristics will still exist; however, the intensity of those characteristics will increase. Previous generations will continue to struggle with just how different NEOs are and, dare we suggest, might even begin to appreciate Millennials a bit more. Millennials will also face similar struggles with this generation in similar ways that other generations have struggled with Millennials. NEOs may indeed become even more disillusioned with big government and big business, even demanding ethical behavior from those companies they work for and those who govern them. This generation will have had more public exposure to transgender and transsexual individuals than ever before, especially with such a presences as Laverne Cox (*Orange Is the New Black*) and Caitlyn Jenner (formerly known as Bruce Jenner) in the media. NEOs will fight for their right to be who they want to be, even if it makes people uncomfortable. They will also continue to witness, experience, and read about social injustice and will feel more compelled to take action via protests and town meetings. For this generation, Twitter feeds like #BlackLivesMatter and protests in the streets (e.g., Ferguson, Missouri) will become more commonplace. Their sense of community will be challenged by the behaviors of the select few who hold higher status, but their desire for equality and acceptance will guide them in new ways.

Fact or Fiction: NEOs will be confident, cavalier, and committed change agents.

As this generation takes on a larger role within the societal framework, NEOs may indeed step back from the negative perceptions associated with being "cavalier." They will observe how Millennials struggled with this perception and will most likely seek to better understand how others do things. Rest assured that their parents will have scheduled many of their activities, and pressured them to perform well in school given the financial plight they themselves experienced. NEOs will be a confident group to be sure, since their late Gen-Xer and early Millennial parents will encourage them to take risks and offer a safety net in the face of adversity. Most will not expect to live on their own immediately after graduation from high school or college and will nurture relationships with their parents to overcome financial difficulties. College will continue to be viewed as an obstacle to advancement rather than an opportunity for it, especially as the cost of higher education skyrockets. Those who do attend higher education institutions will seek majors with job assurance, especially in the sciences and technological arenas. We will see more young women than ever before finally encouraged to aim high in science, technology, engineering, and mathematics. Loretta Lynch's confirmation as the first African American female Attorney General and head of the Justice Department in 2015 will open doors for many who thought obstacles, both sex and race, could not be overcome. The debates about the right to marry will continue, even though the Supreme Court ruled in favor of same-sex marriage, and more NEOs will embrace difference and take risks earlier than ever before when it comes to their identities.

Despite the growth of diversity, the growing trend for more conservatism, especially religious, will continue to resonate in the public arena. As the country grapples with immigration, trade, foreign policies, education, and other issues, debates will continue to engage the public. NEOs will feel confident in their knowledge of difference and take stands on social issues at a much younger age since their parents and teachers are late Gen-Xers and early Millennials who are more accepting of difference than previous generations. This generation will also be "foot soldiers," mentioned in chapter 4, promoting an agenda of change that this country may have not yet experienced. They will also lead change at the college level as they will see their parents and siblings struggle economically more than other generations, and will demand more from their degree-granting institutions. NEOs may even forego college all together and engage in entrepreneurial ventures more readily. This is likely due to the recognition that the skill sets needed for financial success, in their minds, aren't based solely on a degree, but on access, technological savviness, and confidence. More colleges than ever are starting entrepreneurship majors and minors to target these NEOs while the liberal arts continue to struggle to enroll students. Students will increasingly question the need of the value of any college degree, especially with such a high cost associated with it.

Fact or Fiction: NEOs will still prefer a hands-off leadership style and will demand even less collaboration.

Regarding leadership, we foresee that the NEO preferences for this attribute will not change too drastically from that of the Millennials', but the process in which leadership is established may be different. For example, while many Millennials prefer to have leadership roles rotate given the specific expertise on projects, NEOs may desire more leadership responsibilities sooner and differently, and may actually seek collaboration with others. They will want to work with others and demonstrate their ability, but they will not be happy with giving up that leadership role once it is obtained. Many will want to make leadership decisions and continue to be applauded for their leadership abilities; however, they too will want to be recognized for their success, but small rewards won't work as well. NEOs are projected to have a renewed interest in compensation, especially financial, as workplaces continue to evolve and the scaling of salaries will be based more on merit and success. Those individuals with the appropriate expertise and training will find themselves restricted in workplace advancement and the gap in salaries between lower-level and upper-level workers will decrease, as will the number of jobs. The 2013–2015 minimum wage legislation will provide many NEOs with increased hope for a better future, with or without a degree, but they will also be frustrated and disappointed when the job market is flooded by lesser-skilled workers.

On the contrary, some have even argued that this generation will be less interested in collaborative work because they believe deeply in individuality and creative freedom. Since they often lack interpersonal acuity in many areas, working in small groups or teams can often be frustrating and disappointing for NEOs. The demand for face time on many projects will trouble many NEOs and this challenge will need to be addressed as they age. Their confidence is high, much like their generational predecessors, but frustrations arise more easily, and groups are often not a welcomed sight at school or in the workplace.

Fact or Fiction: A new "C," *customization,* will emerge for NEOs and this will make them more contradistinctive than ever.

The need for customization is absolutely true. NEOs will thrive on customization and may finally become more contradistinctive than their Millennial counterparts. Millennials were essentially the first generation to demand that products and services be directed to them, personally. However, NEOs will demand this even more, not only in the workplace and classroom, but also at home. Advertisers will have to adapt to this and be forward-thinking and aggressive in reaching this generation. NEOs will expect that technology solves every problem and will continue to be the preferred outlet in searching for a solution. If they have a need, then this generation will believe "there's an app for that." If there isn't an app available, then they will have the knowledge and tools to create one for this purpose. Customization will occur at home when each sibling will seek to be different from the others or where children without siblings will demand more technological and personal freedoms. Customization will also take place in the classroom wherein we will experience a call for individualized education in order to assist students in reaching their personal, professional, and academic goals. We are already seeing this at the college level with more colleges hiring "student success counselors." Additionally, customization will happen at work as NEOs will demand ways to be uniquely engaged in every context and will also demand different types of leadership styles from their managers. We may already see this with the holocracy adapted by Zappos. If workplaces won't adapt, then NEOs will make their mark by starting their own businesses and embracing the entrepreneurial spirit.

THE NEXT GENERATION, THE NEXT ERA

As we conclude, we hope that you have discovered ways in which you can work better with people, regardless of their generational "flaws" or "misguided attitudes." What we have offered to the reader are insights into not only who Millennials are, but also who we all are, regardless of when we were born. Generations are different, and will continue to be so, but we know that those differences are influenced by historical events, cultural backgrounds, gender, sex, race, and many other factors; no two people are exactly alike. However, when isolating certain periods in our lives, we can see that similarities do exist between and among generations—at certain times. Children, teenagers, college graduates, parents, and others all exhibit familiar characteristics during their lives related to different life events. All generations have something to be remembered for, and both the NEOs and the Millennials believe that they will be remembered for their tech-savviness and technological advancements. At the end of the day, the NEOs aren't too far away from making their mark. We need to embrace their differences and abilities, and help them succeed as best as possible, just as previous generations helped us do the same.

NOTES

1. TRADITIONALISTS, BABY BOOMERS, GENERATION-X

1. Robert G. DelCampo, *Managing the Multi-generational Workforce from the GI Generation to the Millennials* (Farnham, UK: Gower, 2010).

2. Neil Howe and William Strauss, "From Babies on Board to Power Teens," in *Millennials Rising: The Next Great Generation* (New York: Vintage Books, 2000), 31–58.

3. Ibid.

4. DelCampo, *Managing the Multi-generational Workforce*.

5. "USA QuickFacts from the U.S. Census Bureau," United States Census Bureau, June 8, 2014. Accessed August 14, 2014, from http://quickfacts.census.gov/qfd/states/00000.html.

6. Betty R. Kupperschmidt, "Multigeneration Employees: Strategies for Effective Management," *The Health Care Manager* 19, no. 1 (2000): 65–76, http://www.ncbi.nlm.nih.gov/pubmed/11183655.

7. Frank Giancola, "The Generation Gap: More Myth Than Reality," *Human Resource Planning* 29, no. 4 (2006): 32, http://law-journals-books.vlex.com/vid/generation-gap-more-myth-than-reality-63425083.

8. DelCampo, *Managing the Multi-generational Workforce*.

9. Thom S. Rainer and Jess W. Rainer, *The Millennials: Connecting to America's Largest Generation* (Nashville, TN: B&H, 2011).

10. Ibid.

11. *Events That Shaped the Century* (Alexandria, VA: Time-Life Books, 1998).

12. Douglas Linder, *State v. John Scopes* ("The Monkey Trial"). Accessed August 31, 2014, from http://law2.umkc.edu/faculty/projects/ftrials/scopes/evolut.htm.

13. "America's Historical Documents," National Archives and Records Administration. Accessed August 31, 2014, from http://www.archives.gov/historical-docs/document.html?doc=13&title.raw=the 19th Amendment to the U.S. Constitution: Women's Right to Vote.

14. "Stock Market Crash," *PBS*. Accessed August 31, 2014, from http://www.pbs.org/fmc/timeline/estockmktcrash.htm.

15. "Rosie the Riveter," *History.com*. Accessed August 31, 2014, from http://www.history.com/topics/world-war-ii/rosie-the-riveter.

16. "A Brief History of the Tuskegee Airmen-Red Tail Squadron," *Red Tail Squadron*. Accessed August 31, 2014, from http://www.redtail.org/the-airmen-a-brief-history/

17. "Charles Lindbergh Biography," *Charles Lindbergh: An American Aviator*. Accessed August 31, 2014, from http://www.charleslindbergh.com/history/.

18. DelCampo, *Managing the Multi-generational Workforce*.

19. Nancy Bell and Marvin Narz, "Meeting the Challenges of Age Diversity in the Workplace," *The CPA Journal* 77, no. 2 (2007): http://connection.ebscohost.com/c/articles/23943959/meeting-challenges-age-diversity-workplace.

20. Sheryl Lindsell-Roberts, "Bridging the Multigenerational Divide," in *New Rules for Today's Workplace* (Boston: Houghton Mifflin Harcourt, 2011).

21. United Nations Joint Staff Pension Fund, "Traditionalists, Baby Boomers, Generation X, Generation Y (and Generation Z) Working Together." Accessed June 26, 2015, from http://www.un.org/staffdevelopment/pdf/Designing%20Recruitment,%20Selection%20&%20Talent%20Management%20Model%20tailored%20to%20meet%20UNJSPF's%20Business%20Development%20Needs.pdf.

22. Brent Green, *Marketing to Leading-edge Baby Boomers* (Lincoln, NE: Writers Advantage, 2003).

23. *Events That Shaped a Century*.

24. "Boomers Envision Retirement 2011—AARP," *AARP*, June 1, 2011. Accessed August 14, 2014, from http://www.aarp.org/work/retirement-planning/info-06-2011/boomers-envision-retirement-2011.html.

25. Mary F. Henson, *Trends in the Income of Families and Persons in the United States 1947–1964* (Washington, D.C.: U.S. Department of Commerce, Bureau of the Census, 1967).

26. "History of *Brown v. Board of Education*," *United States Courts*. Accessed August 31, 2014, from http://www.uscourts.gov/educational-resources/

get-involved/federal-court-activities/brown-board-education-re-enactment/history.aspx.

27. John A. Lukacs, *A Short History of the Twentieth Century* (Cambridge, MA: Belknap Press, 2013), 171.

28. Milestones: 1945–1952: Marshall Plan, 1948, *U.S. Department of State Office of the Historian.* Accessed August 31, 2014, from https://history.state.gov/milestones/1945-1952/marshall-plan.

29. "Harry S. Truman," *The White House.* Accessed August 31, 2014, from http://www.whitehouse.gov/about/presidents/harrystruman.

30. Ibid.

31. "Dwight D. Eisenhower," *The White House.* Accessed August 31, 2014, from http://www.whitehouse.gov/about/presidents/dwightdeisenhower.

32. "The Silent Spring," *Natural Resources Defense Council.* Accessed August 28, 2014, from http://www.nrdc.org/health/pesticides/hcarson.asp.

33. Paul Taylor and George Gao, "Generation X: America's Neglected 'Middle Child,'" *Pew Research Center,* June 5, 2014. Accessed August 15, 2014, from http://www.pewresearch.org/fact-tank/2014/06/05/generation-x-americas-neglected-middle-child/.

34. Ann Hulbert, "Look Who's Parenting," *New York Times,* July 4, 2004, http://www.nytimes.com/2004/07/04/magazine/04WWLN.html.

35. "The Silent Spring," *Natural Resources Defense Council.* Accessed August 28, 2014, from http://www.nrdc.org/health/pesticides/hcarson.asp.

36. Paul Taylor and George Gao, "Generation X: America's Neglected 'Middle Child,'" *Pew Research Center,* June 5, 2014. Accessed August 15, 2014, from http://www.pewresearch.org/fact-tank/2014/06/05/generation-x-americas-neglected-middle-child/.

37. Ann Hulbert, "Look Who's Parenting," *New York Times,* July 4, 2004, http://www.nytimes.com/2004/07/04/magazine/04WWLN.html.

38. Susan Gregory Thomas, "A Teacher's Guide to Generation X Parents," *Edutopia,* January 19, 2010. Accessed August 15, 2014, from http://www.edutopia.org/generation-x-parents-relationships-guide.

39. Jeff Gordinier, *X Saves the World: How Generation X Got the Shaft but Can Still Keep Everything from Sucking* (New York: Viking, 2008).

40. "Multigenerational Characteristics," *Bruce Mayhew Consulting.* Accessed August 15, 2014, from http://www.brucemayhewconsulting.com/best-ideas-2/.

41. United Nations Joint Staff Pension Fund, "Traditionalists, Baby Boomers, Generation X, Generation Y (and Generation Z) Working Together." Accessed October 4, 2015, from http://www.un.org/staffdevelopment/pdf/Designing%20Recruitment,%20Selection%20&

%20Talent%20Management%20Model%20tailored%20to%20meet%20UNJS
PF's%20Business%20Development%20Needs.pdf

42. "Backgrounder on the Three Mile Island Accident," *U.S. NRC.* Accessed September 1, 2014, from http://www.nrc.gov/reading-rm/doc-collections/fact-sheets/3mile-isle.html.

43. "Thurgood Marshall Biography," *Bio.com.* Accessed September 1, 2014, from http://www.biography.com/people/thurgood-marshall-9400241.

44. "Miranda Rights." Accessed September 1, 2014, from http://www.mirandarights.org/.

45. *"Roe v. Wade* and Its Impact," *U.S. History: Pre-Colombian to the New Millennium.* Accessed September 1, 2014, from http://www.ushistory.org/us/57d.asp.

46. "The Law," *Equal Employment Opportunity Commission.* Accessed September 1, 2014, from http://www.eeoc.gov/eeoc/history/35th/thelaw/.

47. *After Stonewall,* directed by John Scagliotti (New York: First Run Features, 2005), DVD.

48. *Milk Foundation.* Accessed September 1, 2014, from http://milkfoundation.org/.

49. "Databases, Tables & Calculators by Subject," Bureau of Labor Statistics. Accessed September 1, 2014, from http://data.bls.gov/pdq/SurveyOutputServlet.

50. "Gerald R. Ford," *The White House.* Accessed September 1, 2014, from http://www.whitehouse.gov/about/presidents/geraldford.

51. "James Carter," *The White House.* Accessed September 1, 2014, from http://www.whitehouse.gov/about/presidents/jimmycarter.

52. "Ronald Reagan," *The White House.* Accessed September 1, 2014, from http://www.whitehouse.gov/about/presidents/ronaldreagan.

53. Brian Dunbar, "July 20, 1969: One Giant Leap For Mankind," *NASA.* Accessed September 1, 2014, from https://www.nasa.gov/mission_pages/apollo/apollo11.html.

54. "CHM Revolution," *The Apple II.* Accessed September 1, 2014, from http://www.computerhistory.org/revolution/personal-computers/17/300.

55. Jim McPherson, "Media History Timeline." Accessed September 1, 2014, from http://www.webpages.uidaho.edu/jamm445hart/timeline.htm.

2. WHO ARE MILLENNIALS?

1. Bruce Horovitz, "After Gen X, Millennials, What Should next Generation Be?" *USATODAY.com,* May 4, 2012. Accessed September 22, 2014, from

http://usatoday30.usatoday.com/money/advertising/story/2012-05-03/naming-the-next-generation/54737518/1.

2. Mark Bauerlein, *The Dumbest Generation* (New York: Penguin Group, 2008).

3. Sherry Turkle, *Alone Together* (New York: Basic Books, 2011).

4. Alicia Blain, "The Millenial Tidalwave: Five Elements That Will Change the Workplace of Tomorrow," *Journal of Quality Assurance Institute* 22, no. 2 (April 2008): 11–13.

5. Robert G. DelCampo, Lauren A. Haggerty, Meredith Jane Haney, and Lauren Ashley Knippel, *Managing the Multi-Generational Workforce: From the GI Generation to the Millennials* (Farmer, UK: Gower, 2012).

6. Lindsey Gerdes, *The Best Places to Launch a Career* (New York: McGraw-Hill, 2008).

7. Chuck Underwood, *Generational Imperative: Understanding Generational Differences in the Workplace, Marketplace and Living Room* (Charleston, SC: BookSurge, 2007).

8. Carol Elam, Terry Stratton, and Denise D. Gibson, "Welcoming a New Generation to College: The Millennial Students," *Journal of College Admission* 195 (2007): 20–25. http://cfde.emory.edu/teaching/resourcehubarticle/Welcoming_Millennial_Elam_etal.pdf.pdf.

9. Neil Howe and William Strauss, *Millennials Go to College* (Great Falls, VA: LifeCourse Associates, 2007).

10. DelCampo et al., *Managing the Multi-Generational Workforce*.

11. Ibid.

12. Eddy S. W. Ng, Linda Schweitzer, and Sean T. Lyons, "New Generation, Great Expectations: A Field Study of the Millennial Generation," *Journal of Business and Psychology* 25, no. 2 (2010): 281–292. Accessed from http://www.academia.edu/1410939/New_generation_great_expectations_A_field_study_of_the_millennial_generation.

13. Ron Zemke, Claire Raines, and Bob Filipczak, *Generations at Work: Managing the Clash of Boomers, Gen Xers, and Gen Yers in the Workplace,* 2nd ed. (New York: AMACOM/American Management Association, 2013).

14. "A Portrait of Generation Next," Pew Research Center, February 10, 2010. Accessed June 28, 2015, from http://www.pewsocialtrends.org/files/2010/10/millennials-confident-connected-open-to-change.pdf.

15. Jean M. Twenge, *Generation Me*, revised and updated (New York: Apria Books, 2014).

16. Mark McCrindle, "Understanding Generation Y," *Principal Matters* 55 (2003): 28–31. Accessed from http://search.informit.com.au/documentSummary;dn=200305936;res=IELAPA.

17. Chris Dede, "Planning for 'Neomillennial' Learning Styles: Implications for Investments in Technology and Faculty" (pp. 226–247), in Diana G. Oblinger and James L. Oblinger (Eds.), *Educating the Net Generation* (Boulder, CO: EDUCAUSE, 2003).

18. Ibid.

19. Amanda Lenhart, Mary Madden, and Paul Hitlin, "Teens and Technology: Youth Are Leading the Transition to a Fully Wired and Mobile Nation," Pew Internet & American Life Project, July 27, 2005. Accessed June 28, 2015, from http://www.pewinternet.org/files/old-media/Files/Reports/2005/PIP_Teens_Tech_July2005web.pdf.pdf.

20. Lee S. Shulman, *Teaching as Community Property: Essays on Higher Education* (San Francisco: Jossey-Bass, 2004).

21. Dennis Tapscott, *Grown Up Digital: How the Net Generation is Changing Your World* (New York: McGraw-Hill, 2009).

22. Robert DeBard, "Millennials Coming to College," *New Directions for Student Services 2004*, no. 106 (2004): 33–45. Accessed from http://onlinelibrary.wiley.com/doi/10.1002/ss.123/pdf.

23. Ng et al., "New Generation, Great Expectations."

24. Dimitrios Christakis, "Media and Children," TEDX-Rainier, December 27, 2011. Accessed June 3, 2015, from https://www.youtube.com/watch?v=BoT7qH_uVNo.

25. Marlene Scardamalia and Carl Bereiter, "Knowledge Building: Theory, Pedagogy, and Technology" (pp. 97–118), in R. Keith Sawyer (Ed.), *Cambridge Handbook of the Learning Sciences* (New York: Cambridge University Press, 2006). Accessed from http://ikit.org/fulltext/2006_KBTheory.pdf.

26. Regina Luttrell, "Social Networking Sites in the Public Relations Classroom: A Mixed Methods Analysis of Undergraduate Learning Outcomes Using WordPress, Facebook, and Twitter" (PhD diss., California Institute of Integral Studies, 2012).

27. Chris Dede, "The Evolution of Distance Education: Emerging Technologies and Distributed Learning," *American Journal of Distance Education* 10, no. 2 (1996): 4–36. Accessed from http://eric.ed.gov/?id=EJ534454.

28. Maureen Stout, *The Feel-Good Curriculum: The Dumbing Down of America's Kids in the Name of Self-Esteem* (Boston: Da Capo, 2007).

29. Twenge, *Generation Me*.

30. Howe and Strauss, *Millennials Go to College*.

31. Zemke et al., "Generations at Work."

32. Ibid.

33. Gerdes, "Best Places."

34. "AARP Leading a Multigenerational Workforce," *AARP*. Accessed from http://assets.aarp.org/www.aarp.org_/cs/misc/leading_a_multigenerational_workforce.pdf

35. Ibid.

36. Stephanie Armour, "Generation Y: They've Arrived at Work with a New Attitude," *USATODAY.com*, November 8, 2005. Accessed September 12, 2014, from http://usatoday30.usatoday.com/money/workplace/2005-11-06-gen-y_x.htm.

37. Zemke et al., "Generations at Work."

38. Twenge, *Generation Me*.

39. Ibid.

40. Pew Research Center, "A Portrait of Generation Next."

41. Mark Hugo Lopez, "In 2014, Latinos Will Surpass Whites as Largest Racial/Ethnic Group in California," Pew Research Center, January 1, 2014. Accessed September 29, 2014, from http://www.pewresearch.org/fact-tank/2014/01/24/in-2014-latinos-will-surpass-whites-as-largest-racialethnic-group-in-california/.

42. Ibid.

43. Michael Hais and Morley Winograd, "It's Official: Millennials Realigned American Politics in 2008." *The Huffington Post*, November 17, 2008. Accessed September 5, 2014, from http://www.huffingtonpost.com/michael-hais-and-morley-winograd/its-official-millennials_b_144357.html.

44. David D. Burstein, *Fast Future: How the Millennial Generation Is Shaping Our World* (Boston: Beacon Press, 2013).

45. Pew Research Center, "A Portrait of Generation Next."

46. Neil Howe, "Don't Worry, America: Millennials Still Want to Marry," *Forbes*, March 25, 2014. Accessed September 29, 2014, from http://www.forbes.com/sites/realspin/2014/03/25/dont-worry-america-millennials-still-want-to-marry/.

47. Pew Research Center, "A Portrait of Generation Next."

48. Debard, "Millennials Coming to College."

49. David Kinnaman and Gabe Lyons, *Unchristian: What a New Generation Really Thinks about Christianity—and Why It Matters* (Grand Rapids, MI: Baker Books, 2007).

50. Debard, "Millennials Coming to College."

3. LEADERSHIP: THERE IS AN "I" IN *TEAM*

1. C. S. "Bud" Kulesza and Daniel Smith, "Reverse Mentoring—Something for Everyone!" *Strategic Finance* (April 1, 2013): 21–23, 63. http://www.

thefreelibrary.com/Reverse+mentoring--something+for+everyone!+Reverse+
mentoring+is...-a0326853786.

2. Peter G. Northouse, *Leadership: Theory and Practice*, 6th ed. (Thousand Oaks, CA: Sage, 2013), 2–4.

3. Sherry Penney, "Voices of the Future: Leadership for the 21st Century," *Journal of Leadership Studies* 5, no. 3 (2011): 55–62, doi: 10.1002/jls.20233.

4. Northouse, *Leadership*, 5.

5. Darlene Andert, "Alternating Leadership as a Proactive Organizational Intervention: Addressing the Needs of the Baby Boomers, Generation-Xers and Millennials." *Journal of Leadership, Accountability and Ethics* 8, no. 4 (2011): 67–83. Accessed from http://www.na-businesspress.com/JLAE/Andert84Web.pdf.

6. Jeff R. Hale and Dail L. Fields, "Exploring Servant Leadership across Cultures: A Study of Followers in Ghana and the USA," *Leadership* 3, no. 4 (2007): 397–417. Accessed from http://lea.sagepub.com/content/3/4/397.abstract.

7. Hale and Fields, "Exploring Servant Leadership," 1.

8. "How it Works," *Holocracy*. Accessed June 30, 2015, from http://www.holacracy.org/how-it-works/.

9. "Holocracy and Self-Organization" *Zappos Insights*. Accessed June 30, 2015, from http://www.zapposinsights.com/about/holacracy.

10. Adam Vaccaro, "Why It's So Hard to Turn Fickle Millennials into Leaders," *INC*, March 19, 2014. Accessed October 9, 2014, from http://www.inc.com/adam-vaccaro/young-talent-leadership-development.html.

11. Karen K. Myers and Kamyab Sadaghiani, "Millennials in the Workplace: A Communication Perspective on Millennials' Organizational Relationships and Performance," *Journal of Business Psychology* 25, no. 2 (2010): 225–238. Accessed October 9, 2014, from http://link.springer.com/article/10.1007%2Fs10869-010-9172-7#page-1.

12. Jeanne C. Meister and Karie Willyerd, "Spotlight on Leadership: The Next Generation: Mentoring Millennials," *Harvard Business Review* (May 2010): 1–4. Accessed October 9, 2014, from http://hbr.org/2010/05/mentoring-millennials/.

13. Mark Memmott, "Grad Who Sued Over C+ Grade Flunks in Court," *NPR*. Accessed October 9, 2014, from http://www.npr.org/blogs/thetwo-way/2013/02/15/172098330/grad-who-sued-over-c-grade-flunks-in-court.

14. "Paulo Freire: Dialogue, Praxis, and Education," *Pedagogies for Change*. Accessed October 9, 2014, from http://infed.org/mobi/paulo-freire-dialogue-praxis-and-education/.

15. Jason S. Wrench, *Excellence in Creative Communication*. Accessed June 30, 2015, from http://www.jasonswrench.com/.

16. "Flipped Learning Network," *Flipped Learning.* Accessed October 9, 2014, from http://flippedlearning.org/site/default.aspx?PageID=1.

17. "Funding Opportunities," *Institute of Education Sciences.* Accessed October 9, 2014, http://ies.ed.gov/funding/.

18. "Bloom's Taxonomy," *Bloom's Taxonomy.* Accessed October 9, 2014, from http://www.bloomstaxonomy.org/.

19. Diane Darrow, "K–5 iPad Apps According to Bloom's Taxonomy," *Edutopia.* October 25, 2011. Accessed October 9, 2014, from http://www.edutopia.org/ipad-apps-elementary-blooms-taxonomy-diane-darrow.

20. "iMovie," *Apple.* Accessed October 9, 2014, from https://www.apple.com/mac/imovie/.

21. "Storyboard Composer," *iTunes Apps.* October 9, 2014, from https://itunes.apple.com/us/app/storyboard-composer/id325697961?mt=8.

22. "ConnectED Initiative," *Whitehouse.* Accessed October 9, 2014, from http://www.whitehouse.gov/issues/education/k-12/connected.

23. Meister and Willyerd, "Spotlight on Leadership," 68.

24. Judy Lindenberger, "Four Tips for Mentoring Millennials," *Workplace Magazine.* Accessed October 9, 2014, from http://www.workplacemagazine.com/ezinestory/HR/2011/April/04262011Article4.shtml.

25. Jan Ferri-Reed, "Leading a Multigenerational Workforce: Three Ways Leaders Can Help Millennials Succeed," *The Journal for Quality & Participation* 35, no.1 (2012): 18–19. Accessed October 9, 2014, from http://asq.org/pub/jqp/past/2012/april/index.html.

26. Derick Stace-Naughton, "The Other Deficit," *Huffington Post: Education,* December 5, 2012. Accessed May 19, 2014, http://www.huffingtonpost.com/derick-stacenaughton/millennials-education-system_b_2317307.html.

27. Andert, "Alternating Leadership," 67–68.

4. CHARACTERISTICS 1 AND 2: CONFIDENT AND CAVALIER

1. Heidi Glenn, "Losing Our Religion: The Growth of the 'Nones," *NPR,* January 13, 2013. Accessed January 12, 2014, from http://www.npr.org/blogs/thetwo-way/2013/01/14/169164840/losing-our-religion-the-growth-of-the-nones.

2. "Cavalier," *Online Etymology Dictionary.* Accessed December 15, 2014, from http://etymonline.com/index.php?term=cavalier.

3. William Strauss and Neil Howe, *Generations: The History of America's Future, 1584 to 2069* (New York: Harper, 1991), 129–130.

4. Ibid., 358–361.

5. "News Release," *Bureau of Labor Statistics*, December 2014. Accessed January 19, 2014, from http://www.bls.gov/news.release/pdf/empsit.pdf.

6. Julie Halpert, "How Millennials Are Saving the Economy," *The Fiscal Times*, May 10 2010. Accessed January 19, 2014, http://www.thefiscaltimes.com/Articles/2012/05/10/How-Millennials-Are-Saving-the-Economy.

7. Ellen McCarthy, "Friendsgiving, a Tradition to Be Thankful For," November 25, 2014. Accessed January 19, 2015, from http://www.washingtonpost.com/lifestyle/style/friendsgiving-a-new-tradition-to-be-thankful-for/2014/11/25/66aab37a-74b6-11e4-a755-e32227229e7b_story.html.

8. "Millennials in Adulthood," *Pew Social Trends*, March 7, 2014. Accessed January 19, 2015, from http://www.pewsocialtrends.org/2014/03/07/millennials-in-adulthood/.

9. Paul Taylor and Mark Hugo Lopez, "Six Take-Aways from the Census Bureau's Voting Report," *Pew Research Center*, May 8, 2013. Accessed January 19, 2015, from http://www.pewresearch.org/fact-tank/2013/05/08/six-take-aways-from-the-census-bureaus-voting-report/.

10. "Things You Should Know about . . . Flipped Classrooms," *Educause*, February 2012. Accessed January 26, 2015, from http://net.educause.edu/ir/library/pdf/ELI7081.pdf.

11. Miguel Martinez-Saenz and Steven Schoonover Jr., "Resisting the 'Student-as-Consumer' Metaphor," *AAUP*, November–December 2013. Accessed January 31, 2015, from http://www.aaup.org/article/resisting-student-consumer-metaphor#.VMz5Fi7pX1A.

12. Motley Fool, "The Average American Owes This Much in Student Loan Debt—How Do You Compare?" *NASDAQ*, January 24, 2015. Accessed January 26, 2015, from http://www.nasdaq.com/article/the-average-american-owes-this-much-in-student-loan-debt-how-do-you-compare-cm436200.

5. CHARACTERISTIC 3: CONNECTED

1. "The Changing Brain—Do Digital Natives Really Think Differently?" *Change Music, Insights, Morality & Opinionated*, February 12, 2012. Accessed November 5, 2014, from http://www.chan6es.com/psychology/the-changing-brain-do-digital-natives-really-think-differently.

2. David D. Burstein, *Fast Future: How the Millennial Generation Is Shaping Our World* (Boston: Beacon Press, 2013).

3. Jed Lipinski, "The Legend of The Oregon Trail," *Mental Floss*. Accessed October 20, 2014, from http://mentalfloss.com/article/16758/oregon-trail-apple-ii-edition.

4. "Land of Television," *UShistory.org.* Accessed October 21, 2014, from http://www.ushistory.org/us/53c.asp.

5. Don Tapscott, *Grown Up Digital: How the Net Generation Is Changing Your World* (New York: McGraw-Hill, 2009).

6. Ibid.

7. "Cable Is King but Streaming Stands Strong When It Comes to Americans' TV Viewing Habits," *Harris Interactive: Harris Polls,* June 18, 2014. Accessed October 21, 2014, from http://www.harrisinteractive.com/NewsRoom/HarrisPolls/tabid/447/mid/1508/articleId/1452/ctl/ReadCustomDefault/Default.aspx .

8. Tapscott, *Grown Up Digital.*

9. Kelly West, "Unsurprising: Netflix Survey Indicates People Like To Binge-Watch TV," *Cinema Blend.com,* February 12, 2014. Accessed November 14, 2014, from http://www.cinemablend.com/television/Unsurprising-Netflix-Survey-Indicates-People-Like-To-Binge-Watch-TV-61045.html.

10. Dylan Love, "Why Netflix Is Doubling Down On Original Content, Even If People Aren't Watching It," *International Business Times,* October 3, 2013. Accessed October 21, 2014, from http://www.ibtimes.com/why-netflix-doubling-down-original-content-even-if-people-arent-watching-it-1698798.

11. Kirsten Acuna, "Here's Why Netflix Wants Adam Sandler Even though Critics Trash His Movies," *BusinessInsider,* October 3, 2014. Accessed November 14, 2014, from http://www.businessinsider.com/why-netflix-did-adam-sandler-deal-2014-10.

12. Kurt Abrahamson, "Millennials Are 2X as Likely to Purchase Products They Share About," *ShareThis,* September 23, 2014. Accessed October 21, 2014, from http://www.sharethis.com/blog/2014/09/23/new-consumer-study-millennials-2x-likely-purchase-products-share/#sthash.F1tbzL71.QgbPklhg.dpbs.

13. West, "Unsurprising."

14. Ibid.

15. "The Changing Brain."

16. Matt Hamblen, "Consumer Tech Key in Boston Marathon Bombing Probe," *Computerworld,* April 20, 2013. Accessed October 22, 2014, from http://www.computerworld.com/article/2496280/mobile-wireless/consumer-tech-key-in-boston-marathon-bombing-probe.html.

17. Simon Rogers, "The Boston Bombing: How Journalists Used Twitter to Tell the Story," *Twitter Blogs,* July 10, 2013. Accessed November 2, 2014.

18. Abrahamson, "Millennials are 2x as Likely."

19. Emily Yahr, "Taylor Swift, Public Relations Genius, Releases 'Out of the Woods' Early," *Washington Post,* October 14, 2014. Accessed October 22,

2014, from http://www.washingtonpost.com/blogs/style-blog/wp/2014/10/14/
taylor-swift-public-relations-genius-releases-out-of-the-woods-early/.

20. Mary Madden et al., "Teens and Technology 2013," *Pew Research Centers Internet American Life Project,* March 13, 2013. Accessed November 2, 2014, from http://www.pewinternet.org/files/oldmedia/Files/Reports/2013/PIP_TeensandTechnology2013.pdf.

21. Ibid.

22. Ibid.

23. Diedre Bannon, "State of Social Media: The Social Media Report," *Pew Research Center RSS,* July 1, 2012. Accessed October 20, 2014, from http://www.nielsen.com/content/dam/corporate/us/en/reports-downloads/2012-Reports/The-Social-Media-Report-2012.pdf.

24. "Special Mobile Advertising Industry Reports," *Millennial Media,* October 1, 2014. Accessed October 23, 2014, from http://www.millennialmedia.com/mobile-intelligence/special-reports/.

25. Cynthia Boris, "A Day in the Life of the Mobile Millennial Mom," *Marketing Pilgrim,* October 28, 2014. Accessed November 14, 2014, from http://www.marketingpilgrim.com/2014/10/a-day-in-the-life-of-the-mobile-millennial-mom.html.

26. Richard Lawson, "How Does Social Media Redefine Friendships and Connections?" *Compukol.com,* August 7, 2014. Accessed November 14, 2014, from http://www.compukol.com/blog/how-does-social-media-redefine-friendships-and-connections/.

27. "Millennials in Adulthood," *Pew Research Centers Social Demographic Trends Project,* March 7, 2014. Accessed October 22, 2014, from http://www.pewsocialtrends.org/2014/03/07/millennials-in-adulthood/.

28. Michelle Castillo, "Millennials Are the Most Stressed Generation, Survey Finds," *CBSNews,* February 13, 2013. Accessed October 22, 2014, from http://www.cbsnews.com/news/millennials-are-the-most-stressed-generation-survey-finds/.

29. Ibid.

30. Ethan Kross et al., "Facebook Use Predicts Declines in Subjective Well-Being in Young Adults," *PLoS ONE* 8, no. 8: e69841, 2013. doi:10.1371/journal.pone.0069841.

31. Burstein, *Fast Future.*

32. Killian Bell, "Apple Plugs Lion in New iPad 2 TV Ad Called 'We'll Always,'" *Cult of Mac,* July 24, 2011. Accessed October 22, 2014, from http://www.cultofmac.com/105911/apple-plugs-lion-in-new-ipad-2-tv-ad-called-well-always/.

33. Diane Mehta, "New Survey Suggests Millennials Have No Idea What Privacy Means," *Forbes,* April 26, 2013. Accessed October 25, 2014, from

http://www.forbes.com/sites/dianemehta/2013/04/26/new-survey-suggests-millennials-have-no-idea-what-privacy-means/.

34. Ibid.

35. Erik Sofge and David Coburn, *Who's Spying on You? The Looming Threat to Your Privacy, Identity, and Family in the Digital Age* (New York: Hearst, 2012).

36. Alice Truong, "Yes, People (Especially Millennials) Are Sharing More Photos and Videos," *Fast Company*, August 28, 2013. Accessed October 25, 2014, from http://www.fastcompany.com/3020659/fast-feed/yes-people-especially-millennials-are-sharing-more-photos-and-video.

37. Sue Bennett, Karl Maton, and Lisa Kervin, "The 'Digital Natives' Debate: A Critical Review of the Evidence," *British Journal of Educational Technology* 39, no. 5 (2007): 775–786.

38. "Changing the Brain."

39. Marc Prensky, "Do They Really Think Differently?" *On the Horizon* 9, no. 6 (2001): 1–6. Accessed from http://www.marcprensky.com/writing/Prensky%20-%20Digital%20Natives,%20Digital%20Immigrants%20-%20Part2.pdf.

40. Ibid., 3.

41. Patricia Marks Greenfield, *Mind and Media: The Effects of Television, Video Games and Computers* (Cambridge, MA: Harvard University Press, 1984).

42. Prensky, "Do They Really Think Differently?", 4.

6. CHARACTERISTIC 4: COLLABORATIVE

1. Kami Dimitrova, "Woman Fired After Tweet on AIDS in Africa Sparks Internet Outrage,"*ABC News: World News*, December 21, 2013. Accessed December 22, 2014, from http://abcnews.go.com/International/woman-fired-tweet-aids-africa-sparks-internet-outrage/story?id=21298519.

2. Edmodo. Accessed from http://www.edmodo.com.

3. Ed Tech Team, "14 Great Facebook Groups Every Teacher Should Know About," *Educational Technology and Mobile Learning.* Accessed December 22, 2014, from http://www.educatorstechnology.com/2012/11/14-great-facebook-groups-every-teacher.html.

4. Anonymous, personal communication, January 2015. Person doesn't want to be identified.

7. CHARACTERISTICS 5 AND 6:
COMMITTED CHANGE AGENTS

1. Forbes Profiles, *Forbes: 400 Issue*. Accessed October 20, 2014, from http://www.forbes.com/sites/forbespr/2014/09/29/forbes-announces-its-33rd-annual-forbes-400-ranking-of-the-richest-americans/.

2. David D. Burstein, *Fast Future: How the Millennial Generation Is Shaping Our World* (Boston: Beacon Press, 2013), xi.

3. Elizabeth Holmes, "Theranos Company," *Theranos.com*. Accessed October 20, 2014, from http://www.theranos.com.

4. Adam Vincenzini, "The 7 Types of Social Media Specialists," *PR Daily*. Accessed October 20, 2014, from http://www.prdaily.com/Main/Articles/The_7_types_of_social_media_specialists_14183.aspx.

5. "Open Doors 2013," *Institute of International Education*. Accessed October 23, 2014, from http://www.iie.org/Research-and-Publications/Open-Doors.

6. "Open Doors 2014," *Institute of International Education*. Accessed November 17, 2014, from http://www.iie.org/Research-and-Publications/Open-Doors.

7. "Statistics," *Campus Compact*. Accessed October 23, 2014, from http://www.compact.org/about/statistics/.

8. Ibid.

9. Paulo Freire,` *Pedagogy of the Oppressed* (New York: Herder and Herder, 1970).

10. Allison Jordan, "Know Your Audience: 12 Key Insights for Different Ages in the Digital Sphere," *Word of Mouth Marketing Association*. Accessed October 30, 2014, from http://www.womma.org/posts/2013/12/know-your-audience-12-key-insights-for-different-ages-in-the-digital-sphere.

11. " The Flipped Classroom: Turning Teaching on its Head," *Knewton*. Accessed October 30, 2014, from http://www.knewton.com/flipped-classroom/.

12. "Catchphrases, Expressions, and Slogans of the '50s–'60s–'70s–'80s," *Wordpress*, June 9, 2009. Accessed October 23, 2014, from http://coolrain44.wordpress.com/2009/06/09/slogans-catchphrases-of-the-60s-70s-80s/.

13. "Pentagon Papers," *The National Archive*. Accessed October 23, 2014, from http://www.archives.gov/research/pentagon-papers/.

14. "Watergate: The Scandal That Brought Down Richard Nixon," *Watergate.info*. Accessed October 23, 2014, from http://watergate.info.

15. David Carr, "How Obama Tapped into Social Networks' Power, *New York Times: Media & Advertising*, November 10, 2008. Accessed October 23, 2014, from http://www.nytimes.com/2008/11/10/business/media/10carr.html?_r=0.

16. Pew Research Journalism Project, "How the Presidential Candidates Use the Web and Social Media," *Journalism.org*, August 15, 2012. Accessed October 23, 2014, from http://www.journalism.org/2012/08/15/how-presidential-candidates-use-web-and-social-media/.

17. #OCCUPYTOGETHER. Accessed October 24, 2014, from http://www.occupytogether.org/.

18. "Financial Information 2014," *ALS Organization*. Accessed October 24, 2014, from http://www.alsa.org/about-us/financial-information.html.

19. Pablo Barberá and Megan Metzger, "Tweeting the Revolution: Social Media Use and the #Euromaidan Protests," *Huffington Post: Politics,* April 23, 2014. Accessed October 24, 2104, from http://www.huffingtonpost.com/pablo-barbera/tweeting-the-revolution-s_b_4831104.html, para. 2.

20. Jeff Widener, "The Big Picture," *Boston.com*. Accessed October 24, 2014, http://www.boston.com/bigpicture/2014/06/25th_anniversary_of_the_tiananmen_square_mass.html.

21. Robbie Couch, "87% of Millennials Donated to Charity Last Year and You Should Stop Calling Them Selfish: Report," *Huffington Post,* June 19, 2014. Accessed October 30, 2014, from http://www.huffingtonpost.com/2014/06/18/millennials-volunteer-charity-giving_n_5507778.html.

22. Elaine Yu, "How Millennials Are Changing the Workplace—for Good," *PND Blog: Philantopic,* June 23, 2014. Accessed October 30, 2014, from http://www.pndblog.typepad.com, para 3.

23. Stacey Winconek, "Kyle Smitley: Founder of Detroit Achievement Academy," *Metroparent,* April 1, 2014. Accessed October 31, 2014, from http://www.metroparent.com/Metro-Parent/April-2014/Kyle-Smitley-Founder-of-Detroit-Achievement-Academy/.

24. "What," *EPHAS*. Accessed October 31, 2014, from http://www.ephas.org/index.php/ct-menu-item-5.

25. Lynne Klaft, "Power through Photos," *Telegram,* August 11, 2010. Accessed October 31, 2014, from http://www.telegram.com/article/20100811/NEWS/8110377/1101/rss01&source=rss.

26. "About Us," *Clarity Project*. Accessed October 31, 2014, from http://www.clarityproject.com/.

27. Bradley Depew, "How Millennials Are Changing Charitable Giving," *About.com*. Accessed October 15, 2014, from http://nonprofit.about.com/od/fordonors/a/How-Millennials-Are-Changing-Charitable-Giving.htm.

28. Derrick Feldmann, "How Millennials Are Changing the Definition of 'Philanthropy,'" *Case Foundation,* February 12, 2014. Accessed October 15, 2014, from http://casefoundation.org/blog/millennials-changing-definition-philanthropy.

29. Derrick Feldmann and Ted Grossnickle, "Millennial Donors: A Study of Millennial Giving and Engagement Habits," *CDN.trustedpartner.com*. Accessed October 15, 2014, from http://cdn.trustedpartner.com/docs/library/AchieveMCON2013/MD10%20Full%20Report.pdf.

8. CHARACTERISTIC 7: CONTRADISTINCTIVE

1. Alyssa Morones, "Corporal Punishment Persists in Some US Schools," *Education Week*, October 24, 2013. Accessed March 3, 2015, from http://www.edweek.org/ew/articles/2013/10/23/09spanking_ep.h33.html.

2. Pat Borzi and Steve Eder, "Vikings' Adrian Peterson Booked on Charge of Child Abuse," *New York Times*, September 14, 2014. Accessed March 3, 2015, from http://www.nytimes.com/2014/09/14/sports/vikings-peterson-is-booked-on-charge-of-child-abuse.html?_r=0.

3. Neil Howe and William Strauss, *Generations: The History of America's Future, 1584 to 2069* (New York: William Morrow Company, 1992).

4. "Selma to Montgomery March," *History.* Accessed March 16, 2015, from http://www.history.com/topics/black-history/selma-montgomery-march.

5. "Kent State Incident," *History,* accessed March 16, 2015, http://www.history.com/topics/vietnam-war/kent-state.

6. Susan Cain, *Quiet: The Power of Introverts in a World that Can't Stop Talking* (New York: Random House, 2012).

7. Jane McManus, "Curt Schilling, Unlikely Internet Vigilante," *ESPNW*, March 4, 2015. Accessed April 2, 2015, from http://espn.go.com/espnw/news-commentary/article/12418373/curt-schilling-unlikely-internet-vigilante.

8. Cain, *Quiet*.

9. "McCarthyism," *US History: Pre-Columbian to the New Millennium.* Accessed April 4, 2015, from http://www.ushistory.org/us/53a.asp.

10. The Leadership Conference, "The Stonewall Riots: The Beginning of the LGBT Movement," *CivilRights.org,* June 9, 2009. Accessed March 16, 2015, from http://www.civilrights.org/archives/2009/06/449-stonewall.html.

11. Julie Scelfo, "A University Recognizes a Third Gender: Neutral," *New York Times,* February 3, 2015. Accessed from http://www.nytimes.com/2015/02/08/education/edlife/a-university-recognizes-a-third-gender-neutral.html?_r=0.

12. College Equality Index, "List of Colleges with Gender Neutral Housing." Accessed March 16, 2015, from http://www.collegeequalityindex.org/list-colleges-gender-neutral-housing .

13. Kim Bellware, "Gender-neutral Bathrooms Are Quietly Becoming the New Thing at Colleges," *Huffington Post,* July 18, 2014. Accessed March 16,

2015, from http://www.huffingtonpost.com/2014/07/18/gender-neutral-bathrooms-colleges_n_5597362.html.

14. Domenico Montanaro, "Indiana Law: Sorting Fact from Fiction," *NPR*, April 1, 2015. Accessed April 2, 2015, from http://www.npr.org/blogs/itsallpolitics/2015/04/01/395613897/sorting-fact-from-fiction-from-politics-on-the-indiana-law.

15. "Investigation Underway After Noose Found on Duke Campus," WRAL.com, April 1, 2015. Accessed April 2, 2015, from http://www.wral.com/investigation-underway-after-noose-found-on-duke-campus/14553047/.

16. Upstart, "Modern Families: The Divorce Rate Is Lower but the Myth Lives On," *New York Times,* December 2, 2014. Accessed March 16, 2015, from http://www.nytimes.com/2014/12/02/upshot/the-divorce-surge-is-over-but-the-myth-lives-on.html?_r=0&abt=0002&abg=1.

17. "An Overview of Second-wave Feminism," *Women's History.* Accessed March 16, 2015, from http://womenshistory.answers.com/feminism/an-overview-of-second-wave-feminism.

18. "Mental Health Surveillance Among Children—United States, 2005–2011," *Center for Disease Control,* May 17, 2013. Accessed March 19, 2015, from http://www.cdc.gov/mmwr/preview/mmwrhtml/su6202a1.htm.

BIBLIOGRAPHY

"A Brief History of the Tuskegee Airmen—Red Tail Squadron." *Red Tail Squadron.* Accessed August 31, 2014, from http://www.redtail.org/the-airmen-a-brief-history/.

"A Portrait of Generation Next." *Pew Research Center.* February 10, 2010. Accessed June 28, 2015, from http://www.pewsocialtrends.org/files/2010/10/millennials-confident-connected-open-to-change.pdf.

"About Us." *Clarity Project.* Accessed October 31, 2014, from http://www.clarityproject.com/

Abrahamson, Kurt. "Millennials are 2X as Likely to Purchase Products They Share About." *ShareThis,* September 23, 2014. Accessed October 21, 2014, from http://www.sharethis.com/blog/2014/09/23/new-consumer-study-millennials-2x-likely-purchase-products-share/#sthash.F1tbzL71.QgbPklhg.dpbs.

Acuna, Kirsten. "Here's Why Netflix Wants Adam Sandler Even though Critics Trash His Movies." *BusinessInsider,* October 3, 2014. Accessed November 14, 2014, from http://www.businessinsider.com/why-netflix-did-adam-sandler-deal-2014-10.

After Stonewall. Directed by John Scagliotti. New York: First Run Features, 2005. View a description at http://www.imdb.com/title/tt0244955/combined.

"America's Historical Documents." *National Archives and Records Administration.* Accessed August 31, 2014, from http://www.archives.gov/historicaldocs/document.html?doc=13&title.raw=19th+Amendment+to+the+U.S.+Constitution:+Women%27s+Right+to+Vote.

"An Overview of Second-Wave Feminism." *Women's History.* Accessed March 16, 2015, from http://womenshistory.answers.com/feminism/an-overview-of-second-wave-feminism.

Andert, Darlene. "Alternating Leadership as a Proactive Organizational Intervention: Addressing the Needs of the Baby Boomers, Generation Xers and Millennials." *Journal of Leadership, Accountability and Ethics* 8, no. 4 (2011): 67–83. Accessed from http://www.na-businesspress.com/JLAE/Andert84Web.pdf.

Armour, Stephanie. "Generation Y: They've Arrived at Work with a New Attitude." *USA TODAY,* November 8, 2005. Accessed September 12, 2014, from http://usatoday30.usatoday.com/money/workplace/2005-11-06-gen-y_x.htm.

Armstrong, Patricia. "Bloom's Taxonomy." *Vanderbilt University: Center for Teaching.* Accessed October 30, 2014, from http://cft.vanderbilt.edu/guides-sub-pages/blooms-taxonomy/.

"Baby Boomers Envision Retirement What's Next?" *AARP,* June 1, 2011. Accessed August 14, 2014, from http://www.aarp.org/work/retirement-planning/info-06-2011/boomers-envision-retirement-2011.html.

"Backgrounder on the Three Mile Island Accident." *U.S. NRC*. Accessed September 1, 2014, from http://www.nrc.gov/reading-rm/doc-collections/fact-sheets/3mile-isle.html.

Bannon, Diedre. "State of Social Media: The Social Media Report." *Pew Research Center*, July 1, 2012. Accessed October 20, 2014, from http://www.nielsen.com/content/dam/corporate/us/en/reports-downloads/2012-Reports/The-Social-Media-Report-2012.pdf.

Barberá, Pablo, and Megan Metzger. "Tweeting the Revolution: Social Media Use and the #Euromaidan Protests," *Huffington Post: Politics*, April 23, 2014. Accessed October 24, 2014, from http://www.huffingtonpost.com/pablo-barbera/tweeting-the-revolution-s_b_4831104.html, para. 2.

Bauerlein, Mark. *The Dumbest Generation*. New York: Penguin Group, 2008.

Beattie, Andrew. "Market Crashes: The Dotcom Crash," *Investopedia*. Accessed October 9, 2014, from http://www.investopedia.com/features/crashes/crashes8.asp.

Bell, Killian. "Apple Plugs Lion in New iPad 2 TV Ad Called 'We'll Always.'" *Cult of Mac*, July 24, 2011. Accessed October 22, 2014, from http://www.cultofmac.com/105911/apple-plugs-lion-in-new-ipad-2-tv-ad-called-well-always/.

Bell, Nancy, and Marvin Narz. "Meeting the Challenges of Age Diversity in the Workplace." *The CPA Journal* 77, no. 2 (2007), http://connection.ebscohost.com/c/articles/23943959/meeting-challenges-age-diversity-workplace.

Bellware, Kim. "Gender-neutral Bathrooms Are Quietly Becoming the New Thing at Colleges." *Huffington Post*, July 18, 2014. Accessed March 16, 2015, from http://www.huffingtonpost.com/2014/07/18/gender-neutral-bathrooms-colleges_n_5597362.html.

Bennett, Sue, Karl Maton, and Lisa Kervin, "The 'Digital Natives' Debate: A Critical Review of the Evidence." *British Journal of Educational Technology* 39, no. 5 (2007): 775–786. Accessed from http://ro.uow.edu.au/cgi/viewcontent.cgi?article=2465&context=edupapers.

Blain, Alicia. "The Millennial Tidalwave: Five Elements That Will Change the Workplace of Tomorrow." *Quality Assurance Institute Worldwide* (April 2008): 11–13.

"Bloom's Taxonomy." Accessed October 9, 2014, from http://www.bloomstaxonomy.org/.

"Boomers Envision Retirement 2011." *AARP*. June 1, 2011. Accessed August 14, 2014, from http://www.aarp.org/work/retirement-planning/info-06-2011/boomers-envision-retirement-2011.html.

Boris, Cynthia. "A Day in the Life of the Mobile Millennial Mom." *Marketing Pilgrim*, October 28, 2014. Accessed November 14, 2014, from http://www.marketingpilgrim.com/2014/10/a-day-in-the-life-of-the-mobile-millennial-mom.html.

Borzi, Pat, and Steve Eder. "Vikings' Adrian Peterson Booked on Charge of Child Abuse." *New York Times*, September 13, 2014. Accessed March 3, 2015, from http://www.nytimes.com/2014/09/14/sports/vikings-peterson-is-booked-on-charge-of-child-abuse.html?_r=0.

Burstein, David. "18 in '08." Vimeo.com. Accessed October 20, 2014, from http://vimeo.com/59426707.

Burstein, David D. *Fast Future: How the Millennial Generation Is Shaping Our World*. Boston: Beacon Press, 2013.

"Cable Is King But Streaming Stands Strong When It Comes to Americans' TV Viewing Habits." *Harris Interactive: Harris Polls*. June 18, 2014. Accessed October 21, 2014, from http://www.harrisinteractive.com/NewsRoom/HarrisPolls/tabid/447/mid/1508/articleId/1452/ctl/ReadCustom Default/Default.aspx.

Cain, Susan. *Quiet: The Power of Introverts in a World that Can't Stop Talking*. New York: Random House, 2012.

"Carol Gilligan." *Ethicsofcare.org*, June 1, 2011. Accessed October 30, 2014, from http://ethicsofcare.org/interviews/carol-gilligan/.

Carr, David. "How Obama Tapped into Social Networks' Power." *New York Times: Media & Advertising*, November 10, 2008. Accessed October 23, 2014, from http://www.nytimes.com/2008/11/10/business/media/10carr.html?_r=0.

Castillo, Michelle. "Millennials are the Most Stressed Generation, Survey Finds," *CBS News*, February 13, 2013. Accessed October 22, 2014, from http://www.cbsnews.com/news/millennials-are-the-most-stressed-generation-survey-finds/.

"Catchphrases, Expressions, and Slogans of the '50s–'60s–'70s–'80s." *Wordpress,* June 9, 2009. Accessed October 23, 2014, from http://coolrain44.wordpress.com/2009/06/09/slogans-catchphrases-of-the-60s-70s-80s/.

"Cavalier." *Online Etymology Dictionary.* Accessed December 15, 2014, from http://etymonline.com/index.php?term=cavalier.

"The Changing Brain—Do Digital Natives Really Think Differently?" *Change Music, Insights, Morality & Opinionated,* February 12, 2012. Accessed November 5, 2014, from http://www.chan6es.com/psychology/the-changing-brain-do-digital-natives-really-think-differently.

"Charles Lindbergh Biography." Accessed August 31, 2014, from http://www.charleslindbergh.com/history/.

"CHM Revolution." The Apple II. Accessed September 1, 2014, from http://www.computerhistory.org/revolution/personal-computers/17/300.

Christakis, Dimitrios. "Media and Children." TEDX-Rainier, Dec 27, 2011. Accessed June 3, 2015, from https://www.youtube.com/watch?v=BoT7qH_uVNo.

College Equality Index. "List of Colleges with Gender Neutral Housing." Accessed March 16, 2015, from http://www.collegeequalityindex.org/list-colleges-gender-neutral-housing.

"ConnectED Initiative." *Whitehouse.* Accessed October 9, 2014, from http://www.whitehouse.gov/issues/education/k-12/connected.

Couch, Robbie. "87% of Millennials Donated to Charity Last Year and You Should Stop Calling Them Selfish: Report." *Huffington Post,* June 18, 2014. Accessed October 30, 2014, from http://www.huffingtonpost.com/. 2014/06/18/millennials-volunteer-charity-giving_n_5507778.html.

Darrow, Diane. "K-5 iPad Apps According to Bloom's Taxonomy." *Edutopia.* October 25, 2011. Accessed October 9, 2014, from http://www.edutopia.org/ipad-apps-elementary-blooms-taxonomy-diane-darrow.

"Databases, Tables and Calculators by Subject." *Bureau of Labor Statistics.* Accessed September 1, 2014, from http://data.bls.gov/pdq/SurveyOutputServlet.

DeBard, Robert. "Millennials Coming to College." *New Directions for Student Services* 2004 no. 106 (2004): 33–45. View the abstract at http://onlinelibrary.wiley.com/doi/10.1002/ss.123/abstract.

Dede, Chris. "Planning for 'Neomillennial' Learning Styles: Implications for Investments in Technology and Faculty." In *Educating the Net Generation,* edited by J. Oblinger and D. Oblinger, 226–247. Boulder, CO: EDUCAUSE, 2003.

———. "The Evolution of Distance Education: Emerging Technologies and Distributed Learning." *American Journal of Distance Education* 10, no. 2 (1996): 4–36.

DelCampo, Robert G., Meredith Jane Haney, Lauren A. Haggerty, and Lauren Ashley Knippel. *Managing the Multi-Generational Workforce: From the GI Generation to the Millennials.* Farnham, UK: Gower Publishing, 2010.

Depew, Bradley. "How Millennials are Changing Charitable Giving." *About.com.* Accessed October 15, 2014, from http://nonprofit.about.com/od/fordonors/a/How-Millennials-Are-Changing-Charitable-Giving.htm.

Dimitrova, Kami. "Woman Fired after Tweet on AIDS in Africa Sparks Internet Outrage." *ABC News: World News,* December 21, 2013. Accessed December 22, 2014, from http://abcnews.go.com/International/woman-fired-tweet-aids-africa-sparks-internet-outrage/story?id=21298519.s.

Dunbar, Brian. "July 20, 1969: One Giant Leap for Mankind." *NASA.* Accessed September 1, 2014, from https://www.nasa.gov/mission_pages/apollo/apollo11.html.

"Dwight D. Eisenhower." *The White House.* Accessed August 28, 2014, from http://www.whitehouse.gov/about/presidents/dwightdeisenhower.

Ed Tech Team, "14 Great Facebook Groups Every Teacher Should Know About." *Educational Technology and Mobile Learning.* Accessed December 22, 2014, from http://www.educatorstechnology.com/2012/11/14-great-facebook-groups-every-teacher.html.

Elam, Carol, Terry Stratton, and Denise D. Gibson. "Welcoming a New Generation to College: The Millennial Students." *Journal of College Admission* 195 (2007): 20–25.

Events That Shaped the Century. Alexandria, VA: Time-Life Books, 1998.

Feldmann, Derrick. "How Millennials are Changing the Definition of 'Philanthropy.'" *Case Foundation,* February 12, 2014. Accessed October 15, 2014, from http://casefoundation. org/blog/millennials-changing-definition-philanthropy.

Feldmann, Derrick, and Ted Grossnickle. "Millennial Donors: A Study of Millennial Giving and Engagement Habits." *CDN.trustedpartner.com.* Accessed October 15, 2014, from http://cdn.trustedpartner.com/docs/library/AchieveMCON2013/ MD10%20Full%20Report.pdf.

Ferri-Reed, Jan. "Leading a Multigenerational Workforce: Three Ways Leaders Can Help Millennials Succeed." *The Journal for Quality & Participation* 35, no. 1 (2012): 18–19. Accessed October 9, 2014, from http://asq.org/pub/jqp/past/2012/april/index.html.

"Financial Information 2014." *ALS Organization.* Accessed October 24, 2014, from http:// www.alsa.org/about-us/financial-information.html.

"The Flipped Classroom: Turning Teaching on Its Head." *Knewton.* Accessed October 30, 2014, from http://www.knewton.com/flipped-classroom/.

"Flipped Learning Network." Accessed October 9, 2014, from http://flippedlearning.org/site/ default.aspx?PageID=1.

Fool, Motley. "The Average American Owes This Much in Student Loan Debt—How Do You Compare?" *Nasdaq.* January 24, 2015. Accessed January 26, 2015, from http://www. nasdaq.com/article/the-average-american-owes-this-much-in-student-loan-debt-how-do-you-compare-cm436200.

Forbes Profiles. *Forbes: 400 Issue,* October 20, 2014, from http://www.forbes.com/sites/ forbespr/2014/09/29/forbes-announces-its-33rd-annual-forbes-400-ranking-of-the-richest-americans/.

Freire, Paulo. *Pedagogy of the Oppressed.* New York: Herder and Herder, 1970.

"Funding Opportunities." *Institute of Education Sciences.* Accessed October 9, 2014, from http://ies.ed.gov/funding/.

"Generation 18." *Generation18.com.* Accessed October 20, 2014, from http://generation18. com/.

"Gerald R. Ford." *The White House.* Accessed September 1, 2014, from http://www. whitehouse.gov/about/presidents/geraldford.

Gerdes, Lindsey. *The Best Places to Launch a Career.* New York: McGraw-Hill, 2008.

Giancola, Frank. "The Generation Gap: More Myth than Reality." *Human Resource Planning* 29, no. 4 (2006): 32. Accessed from http://law-journals-books.vlex.com/vid/ generation-gap-more-myth-than-reality-63425083.

Glenn, Heidi. "Losing Our Religion: The Growth of the 'Nones,'" *NPR.* January 13, 2013. Accessed January 12, 2014, from http://www.npr.org/blogs/thetwo-way/2013/01/14/ 169164840/losing-our-religion-the-growth-of-the-nones.

Gordinier, Jeff. *X Saves the World: How Generation X Got the Shaft but Can Still Keep Everything from Sucking.* New York: Viking, 2008.

Green, Brent. *Marketing to Leading-edge Baby Boomers.* Lincoln, NE: Writers Advantage, 2003.

Greenfield, Patricia Marks. *Mind and Media: The Effects of Television, Video Games and Computers.* Cambridge, MA: Harvard University Press, 1984.

Hais, Michael, and Morley Winograd. "It's Official: Millennials Realigned American Politics in 2008." *Huffington Post,* November 17, 2008. Accessed September 5, 2014, from http:// www.huffingtonpost.com/michael-hais-and-morley-winograd/its-official-millennials_b_ 144357.html.

Hale, Jeff R., and Dail L. Fields. "Exploring Servant Leadership across Cultures: A Study of Followers in Ghana and the USA." *Leadership* 3, no. 4 (2007): 397–417. Accessed from http://lea.sagepub.com/content/3/4/397.abstract.

Halpert, Julie. "How Millennials Are Saving the Economy." *The Fiscal Times.* May 10, 2010. Accessed January 19, 2014, from http://www.thefiscaltimes.com/Articles/2012/05/10/ How-Millennials-Are-Saving-the-Economy.

Hamblen, Matt. "Consumer Tech Key in Boston Marathon Bombing Probe." *Computerworld,* April 20, 2013. Accessed October 22, 2014, from http://www.computerworld.com/

article/2496280/mobile-wireless/consumer-tech-key-in-boston-marathon-bombing-probe. html.

"Harry S. Truman." *The White House.* Accessed August 31, 2014, from http://www. whitehouse.gov/about/presidents/harrystruman.

Henson, Mary F. *Trends in the Income of Families and Persons in the United States 1947–1964.* U.S. Department of Commerce: Bureau of the Census, 1967.

"History of Alternative Energy and Fossil Fuels." Alternative Energy—ProCon.org. Accessed September 1, 2014, from http://alternativeenergy.procon.org/view.timeline.php? timelineID=000015#1951-1999.

"History of *Brown v. Board of Education.*" *United States Courts.* Accessed August 31, 2014, from http://www.uscourts.gov/educational-resources/get-involved/federal-court-activities/ brown-board-education-re-enactment/history.aspx.

Holmes, Elizabeth. "Theranos Company." *Theranos.com.* Accessed October 20, 2014, from http://www.theranos.com.

"Holocracy and Self-Organization." *Zappos Insights.* Accessed June 30, 2015, from http:// www.zapposinsights.com/about/holocracy.

Horovitz, Bruce. "After Gen X, Millennials, What Should Next Generation Be?" *USATODAY.com,* May 3, 2012. Accessed September 22, 2014, from http://usatoday30.usatoday. com/money/advertising/story/2012-05-03/naming-the-next-generation/54737518/1.

"How It Works." *Holocracy.* Accessed June 30, 2015 from http://holocracy.org/how-it-works/.

Howe, Neil. "Don't Worry, America: Millennials Still Want To Marry." *Forbes,* March 25, 2014. Accessed September 29, 2014, from http://www.forbes.com/sites/realspin/2014/03/25/dont-worry-america-millennials-still-want- to-marry/.

Howe, Neil, and William Strauss. "From Babies on Board to Power Teens." In *Millennials Rising: The Next Great Generation,* 45. New York: Vintage Books, 2000.

———. *Millennials Go to College.* Great Falls, VA: LifeCourse Associates, 2007.

Hulbert, Ann. "Look Who's Parenting." *New York Times,* July 4, 2004. Accessed June 4, 2015, from http://www.nytimes.com/2004/07/04/magazine/04WWLN.html.

"iMovie." *Apple.* Accessed October 9, 2014, from https://www.apple.com/mac/imovie/.

"Investigation Underway after Noose Found on Duke Campus." *WRAL.* Accessed April 2, 2015, from http://www.wral.com/investigation-underway-after-noose-found-on-duke campus/14553047/.

"James Carter." *The White House.* Accessed September 1, 2014, from http://www. whitehouse.gov/about/presidents/jimmycarter.

"John F Kennedy." *The White House.* Accessed August 28, 2014, from http://www. whitehouse.gov/about/presidents/johnfkennedy.

Jordan, Allison. "Know Your Audience: 12 Key Insights for Different Ages in the Digital Sphere." *Word of Mouth Marketing Association.* Accessed October 30, 2014, from http:// www.womma.org/posts/2013/12/know-your-audience-12-key-insights-for-different-ages- in-the-digital-sphere.

"Kent State Incident." *History.* Accessed March 16, 2015, from http://www.history.com/ topics/vietnam-war/kent-state.

Kinnaman, David, and Gabe Lyons. *Unchristian: What a New Generation Really Thinks about Christianity—and Why It Matters.* Grand Rapids, MI: Baker Books, 2007.

Klaft, Lynne. "Power through Photos." *Telegram.com.* Accessed October 31, 2014, from http://www.telegram.com/article/20100811/NEWS/8110377/1101/rss01&source=rss.

Kross, Ethan, Phillipe Verduyn, Emre Demiralp, Jiyoung Park, David Seungjae Lee, Natalie Lin, Holly Shablack, John Jonides, and Oscar Ybarra. "Facebook Use Predicts Declines in Subjective Well-Being in Young Adults." *PLoS ONE* 8, no. 8 (2013): e69841.

Kulesza, C. S. "Bud," and Daniel Smith. "Reverse mentoring—Something for Everyone!" *Strategic Finance,* April 1, 2013: 21–23, 63. Accessed June 4, 2015, from http://www. thefreelibrary.com/Reverse+mentoring--something+for+everyone!+Reverse+ mentoring+is...-a0326853786.

Kupperschmidt, Betty R. "Multigeneration Employees: Strategies for Effective Management." *The Health Care Manager* 19, no. 1 (2000): 65–76. Accessed from http://www.ncbi. nlm.nih.gov/pubmed/11183655.

"Land of Television," *UShistory.org*. Accessed October 21, 2014, from http://www.ushistory. org/us/53c.asp.

"The Law." *EEOC*. Accessed September 1, 2014, from http://www.eeoc.gov/eeoc/history/ 35th/thelaw/.

Lawson, Richard. "How Does Social Media Redefine Friendships and Connections?" *Compukol.com*. Accessed November 14, 2014, from http://www.compukol.com/blog/how-does-social-media-redefine-friendships-and-connections/.

"Leading a Multigenerational Workforce." *AARP*. Accessed June 3, 2015, from http://assets. aarp.org/www.aarp.org_/cs/misc/leading_a_multigenerational_workforce.pdf.

Lenhart, Amanda, Mary Madden, and Paul Hitlin. "Teens and Technology: Youth Are Leading the Transition to a Fully Wired and Mobile Nation." Washington, DC: Pew Internet & American Life Project. Accessed from http://www.pewinternet.org/files/old-media/Files/ Reports/2005/PIP_Teens_Tech_July2005web.pdf.pdf.

Lindenberger, Judy. "Four Tips for Mentoring Millennials." *Workplace Magazine*, April 4, 2011. Accessed October 9, 2014, from http://www.workplacemagazine.com/ezinestory/ HR/2011/April/04262011Article4.shtml.

Linder, Douglas O. "State v. John Scopes ('The Monkey Trial')." Accessed August 31, 2014, from http://law2.umkc.edu/faculty/projects/ftrials/scopes/evolut.htm.

Lindsell-Roberts, Sheryl. "Bridging the Multigenerational Divide." *New Rules for Today's Workplace*. Boston: Houghton Mifflin Harcourt, 2011.

Lipinski, Jed. "The Legend of the Oregon Trail," *Mental Floss*. Accessed October 20, 2014, from http://mentalfloss.com/article/16758/oregon-trail-apple-ii-edition.

Lopez, Mark Hugo. "In 2014, Latinos Will Surpass Whites as Largest Racial/Ethnic Group in California." *Pew Research Center*. Accessed September 29, 2014, from http://www. pewresearch.org/fact-tank/2014/01/24/in-2014-latinos-will-surpass-whites-as-largest-racialethnic-group-in-california/.

Love, Dylan. "Why Netflix Is Doubling Down On Original Content, Even If People Aren't Watching It." *International Business Times,* October 3, 2013. Accessed October 21, 2014, from   http://www.ibtimes.com/why-netflix-doubling-down-original-content-even-if-people-arent-watching-it-1698798.

Lukacs, John. *A Short History of the Twentieth Century*. Cambridge, MA: Belknap Press, 2013.

Luttrell, Regina. "Social Networking Sites in the Public Relations Classroom: A Mixed Methods Analysis of Undergraduate Learning Outcomes using WordPress, Facebook, and Twitter." PhD Diss., California Institute of Integral Studies, 2012.

"Lyndon B. Johnson." *The White House*. Accessed August 28, 2014, from http://www. whitehouse.gov/about/presidents/lyndonbjohnson.

Madden, Mary, Amanda Lenhart, Maeve Duggan, Sandra Cortesi, and Ura Gasser. "Teens and Technology 2013." *Pew Research Centers Internet American Life Project,* March 13, 2013. Accessed November 2, 2014, from http://www.pewinternet.org/2013/03/13/teens-and-technology-2013/.

"Marshall Plan." *US Department of State: Office of the Historian*. Accessed August 31, 2014, from https://history.state.gov/milestones/1945-1952/marshall-plan.

Martinez-Saenz, Miguel, and Steven Schoonover Jr. "Resisting the 'Student-as-Consumer' Metaphor." *AAUP*. November–December 2014. Accessed January 31, 2015, from http:// www.aaup.org/article/resisting-student-consumer-metaphor#.VMz5Fi7pX1A.

McCarthy, Ellen. "Friendsgiving, a Tradition to Be Thankful for." November 25, 2014. Accessed   January   19,   2015,   from   http://www.washingtonpost.com/lifestyle/style/ friendsgiving-a-new-tradition-to-be-thankful-for/2014/11/25/66aab37a-74b6-11e4-a755-e32227229e7b_story.html.

"McCarthyism." *US History: Pre-Columbian to the New Millennium*. Accessed April 2, 2015, from http://www.ushistory.org/us/53a.asp.

McCrindle, Mark. "Understanding Generation Y." *Principal Matters* 55 (2003): 28–31.

McManus, Jane. "Curt Schilling, Unlikely Internet Vigilante." *ESPNW*, March 4, 2015. Accessed April 2, 2015, from http://espn.go.com/espnw/news-commentary/article/12418373/curt-schilling-unlikely-internet-vigilante.

McPherson, Jim. "Media History Timeline." *University of Idaho*. Accessed September 1, 2014, from http://www.webpages.uidaho.edu/jamm445hart/timeline.htm.

Mehta, Diane. "New Survey Suggests Millennials Have No Idea What Privacy Means." *Forbes*, April 26, 2013. Accessed October 25, 2014, from http://www.forbes.com/sites/dianemehta/2013/04/26/new-survey-suggests-millennials-have-no-idea-what-privacy-means/.

Meister, Jeanne C., and Karie Willyerd. "Spotlight on Leadership: The Next Generation: Mentoring Millennials." *Harvard Business Review*, May 2010: 1–4. Accessed October 9, 2014, from http://hbr.org/2010/05/mentoring-millennials/.

Memmott, Mark. "Grad Who Sued Over C+ Grade Flunks in Court." *NPR.org*. Accessed October 9, 2014, from http://www.npr.org/blogs/thetwo-way/2013/02/15/172098330/grad-who-sued-over-c-grade-flunks-in-court.

"Mental Health Surveillance among Children—United States, 2005–2011." *Center for Disease Control*. Accessed March 19, 2015, from http://www.cdc.gov/mmwr/preview/mmwrhtml/su6202a1.htm.

"Milk Foundation." Accessed September 1, 2014, from http://milkfoundation.org/.

"Millennials: A Portrait of Generation Next." *Pew Research Center*. Accessed from http://www.pewsocialtrends.org/files/2010/10/millennials-confident-connected-open-to-change.pdf.

"Millennials in Adulthood," *Pew Research Centers Social Demographic Trends Project*, March 7, 2014. Accessed October 22, 2014, from http://www.pewsocialtrends.org/2014/03/07/millennials-in-adulthood/.

"Miranda Rights." Accessed September 1, 2014, from http://www.mirandarights.org/.

"Modern Hippie of the Month: Kyle Smitley of Barley and Birch," *Modern Hippie Mag*, January 22, 2010. Accessed October 31, 2014, from http://www.modernhippiemag.com/2010/01/modern-hippie-of-the-month-kyle-smitley-of-barley-birch/.

"The Monkey Trial." *US History: Pre-Columbian to the New Millennium*. Accessed June 2, 2015, from http://www.ushistory.org/us/47b.asp.

Montanaro, Domenico. "Indiana Law: Sorting Fact from Fiction." *NPR*. Accessed April 2, 2015, from http://www.npr.org/blogs/itsallpolitics/2015/04/01/395613897/sorting-fact-from-fiction-from-politics-on-the-indiana-law.

Morones, Alyssa. "Corporal Punishment Persists in Some US Schools." *Education Week*, October 24, 2013. Accessed March 3, 2015, from http://www.edweek.org/ew/articles/2013/10/23/09spanking_ep.h33.html.

"Multigenerational Characteristics." *Bruce Mayhew Consulting*. Accessed August 15, 2014, from http://www.brucemayhewconsulting.com/index.cfm?id=20209.

Myers, Karen K., and Kamyab Sadaghiani. "Millennials in the Workplace: A Communication Perspective on Millennials' Organizational Relationships and Performance." *Journal of Business Psychology* 25, no. 2 (2010): 225–238. Accessed October 9, 2014, from http://link.springer.com/article/10.1007%2Fs10869-010-9172-7#page-1.

"News Release." *Bureau of Labor Statistics*. December 2014. Accessed January 19, 2014, from http://www.bls.gov/news.release/pdf/empsit.pdf.

Ng, Eddy S. W., Linda Schweitzer, and Sean T. Lyons. "New Generation, Great Expectations: A Field Study of the Millennial Generation." *Journal of Business and Psychology* 25, no. 2 (2010): 281–292.

Northouse, Peter G. *Leadership: Theory and Practice*, 6th ed. Thousand Oaks, CA: Sage, 2013.

#OCCUPYTOGETHER. *Occupy Together*. Accessed October 24, 2014, from http://www.occupytogether.org/.

"Open Doors 2013." *Institute of International Education*. Accessed October 23, 2014, from http://www.iie.org/Research-and-Publications/Open-Doors.

"Open Doors 2014." *Institute of International Education*. Accessed November 17, 2014, from http://www.iie.org/Research-and-Publications/Open-Doors.

"Paulo Freire: Dialogue, Praxis, and Education." *Pedagogies for Change.* Accessed October 9, 2014, from http://infed.org/mobi/paulo-freire-dialogue-praxis-and-education/.

Penney, Sherry H. "Voices of the Future: Leadership for the 21st Century." *Journal of Leadership Studies* 5, no. 3 (2011): 55–62.

"Pentagon Papers." *The National Archive.* Accessed October 23, 2014, from http://www.archives.gov/research/pentagon-papers/.

Pew Research Journalism Project. "How the Presidential Candidates Use the Web and Social Media." *Journalism.org.* Accessed October 23, 2014, from http://www.journalism.org/2012/08/15/how-presidential-candidates-use-web-and-social-media/.

Prensky, Marc. "Do They Really Think Differently?" *On the Horizon* 9, no. 6 (2001): 1–6. Accessed from http://www.marcprensky.com/writing/Prensky%20-%20Digital%20Natives,%20Digital%20Immigrants%20-%20Part2.pdf.

Rainer, Thom S., and Jess W. Rainer. *The Millennials: Connecting to America's Largest Generation.* Nashville, TN: B&H Publishing Group, 2011.

"Roe v. Wade and Its Impact." *UShistory.org.* Accessed September 1, 2014, from http://www.ushistory.org/us/57d.asp.

"Ronald Reagan." *The White House.* Accessed September 1, 2014, from http://www.whitehouse.gov/about/presidents/ronaldreagan.

Rogers, Simon. "The Boston Bombing: How Journalists Used Twitter to Tell the Story." July 10, 2013. Accessed November 2, 2014 from https://blog.twitter.com/2013/the-boston-bombing-how-journalists-used-twitter-to-tell-the-story.

"Rosie the Riveter." History.com. Accessed August 31, 2014, from http://www.history.com/topics/world-war-ii/rosie-the-riveter.

Scardamalia, Marlene, and Carl Bereiter. "Knowledge Building: Theory, Pedagogy, and Technology." In *Cambridge Handbook of the Learning Sciences.* Edited by R. Keith Sawyer, 97–118. New York: Cambridge University Press, 2006.

Scelfo, Julie. "A University Recognizes a Third Gender: Neutral," *New York Times,* February 3, 2015. Accessed from http://www.nytimes.com/2015/02/08/education/edlife/a-university-recognizes-a-third-gender-neutral.html?_r=0.

"Selma to Montgomery March," *History.* Accessed March 16, 2015, from http://www.history.com/topics/black-history/selma-montgomery-march.

Shannon-Missa, Larry. "Cable Is King but Streaming Stands Strong When It Comes to Americans' TV Viewing Habits." *Harris Interactive: Harris Polls.* Accessed October 21, 2014, from http://www.harrisinteractive.com/NewsRoom/HarrisPolls/tabid/447/mid/1508/articleId/1452/ctl/ReadCustom Default/Default.aspx.

Shin, Laura. "How to Create the Ideal LinkedIn Profile." *Forbes,* October 20, 2014. Accessed from http://www.forbes.com/sites/laurashin/2014/10/20/how-to-create-the-ideal-linkedin-profile/.

Shulman, Lee S. *Teaching as Community Property: Essays on Higher Education.* San Francisco: Jossey-Bass, 2004.

"The Silent Spring." *Natural Resources Defense Council.* Accessed August 28, 2014, from http://www.nrdc.org/health/pesticides/hcarson.asp.

Sofge, Eric, and David Coburn. *Who's Spying on You?: The Looming Threat to Your Privacy, Identity, and Family in the Digital Age.* New York: Hearst, 2012.

"Special Mobile Advertising Industry Reports," *Millennial Media,* October 1, 2014. Accessed October 23, 2014, from http://www.millennialmedia.com/mobile-intelligence/special-reports/.

Stace-Naughton, Derick. "The Other Deficit," *Huffington Post: Education,* December 5, 2012. Accessed May 19, 2014, from http://www.huffingtonpost.com/derick-stacenaughton/millennials-education-system_b_2317307.html.

"Statistics." *Campus Compact.* Accessed October 23, 2014, from http://www.compact.org/about/statistics/.

"Stock Market Crash." *PBS.* Accessed August 31, 2014, from http://www.pbs.org/fmc/timeline/estockmktcrash.htm.

"The Stonewall Riots: The Beginning of the LGBT Movement." *Civil Rights.org*. Accessed March 16, 2015, from http://www.civilrights.org/archives/2009/06/449-stonewall.html.

"Storyboard Composer." iTunes Apps. Accessed October 09, 2014, from https://itunes.apple.com/us/app/storyboard-composer/id325697961?mt=8.

Stout, Maureen. *The Feel-Good Curriculum: The Dumbing Down of America's Kids in the Name of Self-Esteem*. Boston: Da Capo Press, 2007.

Strauss, William, and Neil Howe. *Generations: The History of America's Future, 1584–2069*. New York: William Morrow & Company, 1992.

Tapscott, D. *Grown Up Digital: How the Net Generation is Changing Your World*. New York: McGraw Hill, 2009.

Taylor, Paul, and George Gao. "Generation X: America's Neglected 'Middle Child.'" *Pew Research Center*, June 5, 2014. Accessed August 15, 2014, from http://www.pewresearch.org/fact-tank/2014/06/05/generation-x-americas-neglected-middle-child/.

Taylor, Paul, and Mark Hugo Lopez. "Six Take-Aways from the Census Bureau's Voting Report." *Pew Research Center*. May 8, 2013. Accessed January 19, 2015, from http://www.pewresearch.org/fact-tank/2013/05/08/six-take-aways-from-the-census-bureaus-voting-report/.

"Things You Should Know about . . . Flipped Classrooms." *Educause*. February 2012. Accessed January 26, 2015, from http://net.educause.edu/ir/library/pdf/ELI7081.pdf.

Thomas, Susan Gregory. "A Teacher's Guide to Generation X Parents." *Edutopia*. Accessed August 15, 2014, from http://www.edutopia.org/generation-x-parents-relationships-guide.

"Thurgood Marshall Biography." *Bio.com*. Accessed September 1, 2014, from http://www.biography.com/people/thurgood-marshall-9400241.

Truong, Alice. "Yes, People (Especially Millennials) Are Sharing More Photos and Videos." *Fast Company*, August 28, 2013. Accessed October 25, 2014, from http://www.fastcompany.com/3020659/fast-feed/yes-people-especially-millennials-are-sharing-more-photos-and-video.

Turkle, Sherry. *Alone Together*. New York: Basic Books, 2011.

Twenge, Jean M. *Generation Me*. New York: Apria Books, 2014.

Underwood, Chuck. *Generational Imperative: Understanding Generational Differences in the Workplace, Marketplace and Living Room*. South Carolina: BookSurge, 2007.

United Nations Joint Staff Pension Fund. "Traditionalists, Baby Boomers, Generation X, Generation Y (and Generation Z) Working Together." *United Nations Joint Staff Pension Fund*. Accessed June 4, 2015, from http://www.un.org/staffdevelopment/pdf/Designing%20Recruitment,%20Selection%20&%20Talent%20Management%20Model%20tailored%20to%20meet%20UNJSPF%27s%20Business%20Development%20Needs.pdf.

Upstart, "Modern Families: The Divorce Rate Is Lower but the Myth Lives On." *New York Times*, December 2, 2014. Accessed March 16, 2015, from http://www.nytimes.com/2014/12/02/upshot/the-divorce-surge-is-over-but-the-myth-lives-on.html?smid=fb-nytimes&smtyp=cur&bicmp=AD&bicmlukp=WT.mc_id&bicmst=1409232722000&bicmet=1419773522000&_r=4&abt=0002&abg=0.

"USA QuickFacts from the US Census Bureau." United States Census Bureau. July 8, 2014. Accessed August 14, 2014, from http://quickfacts.census.gov/qfd/states/00000.html.

Vaccaro, Adam. "Why It's So Hard to Turn Fickle Millennials into Leaders." March 19, 2014. Accessed October 9, 2014, from http://www.inc.com/adam-vaccaro/young-talent-leadership-development.html.

Vincenzini, Adam. "The 7 Types of Social Media Specialists." *PR Daily*, December 30, 2013. Accessed October 20, 2014, from http://www.prdaily.com/Main/Articles/The_7_types_of_social_media_specialists_14183.aspx.

"Watergate: The Scandal That Brought Down Richard Nixon." *Watergate.info*. Accessed October 23, 2014, from http://watergate.info.

West, Kelly. "Unsurprising: Netflix Survey Indicates People Like To Binge-Watch TV." *Cinema Blend.com*. Accessed November 14, 2014, from http://www.cinemablend.com/television/Unsurprising-Netflix-Survey-Indicates-People-Like-Binge-Watch-TV-61045.html.

"What." *EPHAS.org*. Accessed October 31, 2014, from http://www.ephas.org/index.php/ct-menu-item-5.

Widener, Jeff. "The Big Picture." *Boston.com*. Accessed October 24, 2014, from http://www.boston.com/bigpicture/2014/06/25th_anniversary_of_the_tiananmen_square_mass.html.

Winconek, Stacey. "Kyle Smitley: Founder of Detroit Achievement Academy." *Metroparent*, April 1, 2014. Accessed October 31, 2014, from http://www.metroparent.com/Metro-Parent/April-2014/Kyle-Smitley-Founder-of-Detroit-Achievement-Academy/.

Wrench, Jason S. "Basic Biography." *Excellence in Creative Communication*. Accessed June 30, 2015, from http://www.jasonswrench.com/.

Yahr, Emily. "Taylor Swift, Public Relations Genius, Releases 'Out of the Woods' Early." *Washington Post*, October 14, 2014. Accessed October 22, 2014, from http://www.washingtonpost.com/blogs/style-blog/wp/2014/10/14/taylor-swift-public-relations-genius-releases-out-of-the-woods-early/.

Yu, Elaine. "How Millennials Are Changing the Workplace—for Good." *PND Blog: Philantopic*, June 23, 2014. Accessed October 30, 2014, from http://www.pndblog.typepad.com.

Zemke, Ron, Claire Raines, and Bob Filipczak. *Generations at Work Managing the Clash of Boomers, Gen Xers, and Gen Yers in the Workplace*, 2nd ed. New York: AMACOM/American Management Association, 2013.

INDEX

ABOUT THE AUTHORS

Prior to entering the educational field, **Regina (Gina) Luttrell** spent the first half of her career in corporate public relations and marketing. Her extensive background includes strategic development and implementation of public relations and social media, advertising, marketing, and corporate communications. She has led multiple rebranding campaigns, designed numerous websites, managed high-level crisis situations, and garnered media coverage that included hits with the *New York Times*, the CBS Evening News, and the Associated Press. Gina is currently an associate professor of public relations and social media at Eastern Michigan University where she researches, publishes, and discusses public relations, social media, and the Millennial generation's roles both in the classroom and the workforce. Her first book, *Social Media: How to Engage, Share, and Connect*, garnered rave reviews and has been adopted as a valuable resource in many university public relations and social media curricula across the nation.

Karen McGrath (aka Smith) is Professor of Communications at the College of Saint Rose in Albany, New York, where she has been teaching for almost twenty years. She has a passion for learning and enjoys working with students to help them achieve their personal and professional goals. Her interests include general pop culture, comic books, media literacy, gender, and race, with her most recent publications focused on *The Big Bang Theory*'s Sheldon Cooper and an upcoming co-authored book about craft brewing. She hopes to continue to engage each generation to better understand her own.